UNDERSTANDING

Second

Coming

PROPHECY

"A Layman's Point of View"

Doug Rolfe

ISBN-13:

978-0692678169

Cover Design by

Matthew Reese

DEDICATION AND THANKS

This book is dedicated to the memory of my father, Doug Rolfe Sr. He was my mentor and taught me more about the Bible and how to understand it than any other person or instructor that I sat under.

It is very important that I thank my wife Stevie (Stephanie) for spending many countless hours of hard work going over the manuscripts many times to make sure that grammar, spelling, punctuation and understandability of the book were as accurate as possible. Her encouragement and support during this time is invaluable. A total heartfelt thanks to my helpmate of nearly 48 years.

I thank my special friend and supporter Rev. Dan Young for his contribution and direction to my dream of writing a book that could be understood by those who were not trained in seminaries and Bible colleges. His input specifically in chapters 6,7,10, and 11 was beyond what I expected and deserve and I have learned much from him as a result of us working together on this project. Thank you Dan, my brother in Christ.

TABLE OF CONTENTS

TABLE OF CONTENTS PAGE 2

ACKNOWLEDGEMENT

It is an honor to be asked by Doug Rolfe to assist him in writing this book on The Second Coming of Christ. It is a breath of fresh air to see how the church interpreted the second coming until the 1850s when Biblical interpretation was changed to dispensational interpretations and unintentionally to sensationalism. Doug has cut through the maze of wrong teaching on the second coming to return to the historical teachings of the church. He reminds us that Christ does not need a crisis to return because prophecy has been fulfilled and He can return at any moment for those who love and follow Him by faith.

I confess that I have learned more from Doug than he has from me, but hopefully all who read this book will experience what we have experienced: a greater desire to live in such a way that we would be ready to meet the Lord at any time, whether by death or His second coming. Hopefully there will be those who join us in believing in the second coming not because of signs but because Jesus said He would return for us. Let us heed the warning of Christ: "A wicked and adulterous generation asks for a miraculous sign" (Matthew 12:39).

I gave my life to Jesus Christ on January 23rd , 1966 and after forty-three years of pastoral work with my ministry partner and wife Marilyn, I am grateful that God would use us, even if it be in a small way. I share that same sentiment concerning my small input in this book.

I would be amiss if I did not say: "Thank you Stevie for your most gracious hospitality of allowing me to stay in your home, eat your great cooking, and for keeping both Doug and my feet on the ground by your questions.

INTRODUCTION

WHY WRITE ANOTHER BOOK ABOUT PROPHECY

The idea of writing a book about prophecy in the Bible and its effect on us today regarding the future of the church has been on my heart for several years. It seems as though many of the books have been written in such a way as to leave the average lay person in the pew with a lot of terminology that is not clarified or is misunderstood. My goal is to present the material so that it can be easily understood and very readable.

When I asked my dear friend Rev. Dan Young to collaborate with me on this project he graciously said yes. All who read this book will benefit from his wisdom and knowledge. He recently retired after 43 years in the pulpit and is extremely well qualified. His job was to keep me on track with being accurate regarding the study of the Scriptures and my job is to simplify his knowledge for you in a more understandable format.

Growing up on a large farm in south-central Ohio, I learned how critical communication was to getting the job done, understanding that both speaking and receiving the words were important. We could have used large and important sounding words but did we really communicate?

My father taught me that you have not transferred the information until it is understood by the receiver. It can be heard but not understood. My goal with this book is that it will be both heard and clearly understood.

There will be a series of talking points or questions in some of the chapters for you to study with the hope that any area of misunderstanding can be clarified by answering the questions or reviewing the talking points. This book can be used in small group Bible studies, Sunday School classes or simply studied individually.

Having studied second coming prophecy for literally dozens of years, it has become abundantly clear to me that the popular "left behind" teaching is not biblical but is a fictional idea that has been put upon believers as fact, when it really is about as far away from actual prophecy as you can get.

You will find I have repeated some of the points in this book more than once which is being done for emphasis. It is imperative that we glean a clear understanding of the prophecies we are endeavoring to explain as well as the misconceptions by those we believe are in error.

The most important chapters in the book are the five chapters found in section one which I call the milk stool concept. A milk stool has three legs and if any one of them is missing or broken, you cannot use it. So that you can understand why I said that section one is the most critical, I will be addressing the three most important issues that the dispensationalists[1] teach in their second coming prophecy. In fact we will show that you cannot use any of the three legs they try to stand on. The milk stool is broken and you cannot sit on it.

First: They teach that the church will be raptured or lifted out and taken to heaven by a secret coming of the Lord prior to a seven-year tribulation period.

Second: They teach there will be a seven-year tribulation period after the church is gone that will have a devastating effect on the sinners that are "left behind" on this earth.

Third: They teach that Jesus will return with the church, the Christians that have been in heaven with Him, to reign on this earth a thousand years.

We will be addressing all three of these erroneous teachings. There will be repetition regarding these three issues due to the importance of understanding how wrong we believe the dispensationalists are. So if you can see that we have adequately explained where they are in error, as well as what is truth, you will have comprehended the intent of the book. I will be explaining how I believe each of the issues mentioned is being taught in error and will do my best to correctly show what the Bible says about each of these, including when the Lord is going to return and take us to heaven with Him.

I have never believed that, as Christians, we would be

---

[1] See Glossary for the definition

raptured out prior to a Great Tribulation. Even though I had not studied second coming prophecy in great depth initially, it was not until later when I really dug into the evidence of this subject that I began to see even more clearly how off base the pre-tribulation dispensationalists or PTDs[2] were in presenting a "left behind" teaching to an unsuspecting audience. That belief has been incorporated into songs, videos, books, movies and has been accepted by many of the churches as fact.

One reason that it has become so popular is the sensationalism[3] that accompanies the teaching. Also, sorry to say, many Christians have just simply not studied God's Word, but rely on others to teach them what the Bible has to say about everything, including prophecy. My hope and goals are that this book will encourage many believers to dig deeply into the Bible and learn the truths of what God is teaching us.

The majority of today's publications have been presented which lead a reader into thinking that we, as believers, are to be lifted out before some catastrophic event (the supposed Great Tribulation) happens to the world. It is important to understand that this is a recent teaching and is not what the majority of the early church fathers believed and taught. For nearly 1800 years the majority of the church leaders accepted a view that did not include a "lifting out or rapture" of the church prior to a

---

[2] See Glossary for definition of "PTDs"
[3] Ibid "sensationalism"

tribulation on this earth. I find it amazing that this "new truth or enlightenment" has just been revealed in recent years and was not available to the church leaders sooner. It appears to be a lot like what the cults[4] tell us when they say they have received new light or revelations. Granted the pre-tribulation rapture teaching has brought a lot of interest into the last-days thinking ideas, but though it is sensational, it does not necessarily correctly interpret the Word of God concerning end-times prophecy.

I have read through literally dozens of books, researched countless websites, had several discussions and have just simply exhausted many avenues dealing with this subject, as well as have done my best to be true to the Bible and not misinterpret the Word given to us. We will readily admit that the somewhat biased view that we had before starting this project has changed in more than one area. As a result, we will try to present the best possible approach to end times prophecy without being biased.

It is not even remotely possible to write everything that can be covered on this subject in one book.[5] We have tried to cover each area with enough information to at least explain the major points of the material in each chapter. We will be recommending other books and publications for deeper study into each subject addressed here. You will,

---

[4] See Glossary for definition of "cults"

[5] It would take a lifetime to cover all the Bible has to say about end-times prophecy. We have just scratched the surface of this important material with the hope that you will see the truth regarding the Lord's second coming.

however, be given enough information to be able to understand each subject and defend the material taught in this book.

This is not written nor is intended to be viewed as having all the answers to end-times prophecy. We have done the best we can to be faithful to the truth of the Scriptures and our understanding as much as possible. It is with a lot of prayer and hard work that we have dedicated ourselves to this project in the hope that this will cause readers to dig into the Word of God and become more aware of what the Bible really teaches concerning last days prophecy. We will attempt to answer some of the issues that we personally believe are presented in other publications in an erroneous manner and why that is so. We will not take someone's statements and simply address their errors without explaining why we believe they are incorrect and will do so from the Word of God.

Please understand we do not believe that those who see end-times prophecy differently than we do are outside the realm of salvation, but in fact are our brothers in Christ and our differences are not meant to be demeaning to them in any way. We will discuss those differences without malice and hopefully present those issues to better understand God's Word.

For those of you who disagree with the premise of this book we openly welcome sincere dialogue with the understanding that we can disagree about substance, but will not accept personal criticism. It has no place in a

Christian environment and will not be responded to in our social media sites. The media sites will eventually be a face book page for your review and comments as well as a web page for those who wish to order the book and possibly other items we will have for sale. We are not sure about You Tube and Twitter yet.

It is also important to comprehend that we have done our best to not assume what the Scriptures say but have been diligent in finding the truth of what is being presented in God's Word. Sometimes it is not possible to clearly understand what a particular passage may be conveying to us and without further study may miss the real meaning or intent. Thankfully, I had a Bible college professor who taught us that when a passage isn't clear, then go to other verses dealing with the same or similar subject and see what they have to say. In other words, interpret Scripture in light of Scripture. The preponderance of evidence[6] in light of the "whole" of Scripture has been our direction in revealing truth as best we can in this book.

Our goal is to give the reader a fresh and accurate view of prophecy without using a lot of theological terminology.[7] When we do use theological terms, we will define their meaning so there will not be any confusion regarding intent and they will have clarity. There is a glossary at the back of the book with definitions for the terminology used.

---

[6] See Glossary for definition of "Preponderance of Evidence"
[7] See Glossary for "theological terminology"

We have done our best not to plagiarize[8] other writings, as we have spent considerable time in researching several books and publications. If we have made statements that appear similar to what someone else may have made, it is simply an agreement with that statement and is not intended to plagiarize in any way. Much of what we have done is the result of our own time and effort to establish truth the best we can. Where we have directly used other writings, we will acknowledge them.

We pray that God will bless you as you study this material and that it will equip you to share this information with others. It can be a great witnessing tool and open up discussions with your friends and relatives. We trust there will be those who will turn their life to Christ as a result of being exposed to His Word and realize the impact it has on our eternal destination. If you have once been a follower and servant of Christ and walked with Him but have fallen away, may this be a moment in your life where you will be reminded of His soon return and make your way back to a close and personal relationship with the Lord Jesus Christ.

MY PERSONAL TESTIMONY

I wish to share my personal testimony so that you may understand my faith and that I am a true believer in the Bible and its teachings. I believe in the inerrant and infallible Word of God. I believe in the Father, Son, and Holy Spirit, as God three in one or the Trinity. I am saved by the grace

[8] Ibid "plagiarize"

of God according to Ephesians 2:8-9 and understand that Jesus Christ paid for my sins on the cross. John 3:16 tells me that God loved me so much that He gave the ultimate sacrificial gift to secure my redemption. He took my penalty! I have repented of my sins and am doing my best to be obedient to His teachings. I believe that He died on the cross, physically rose again, and is coming back visibly (Acts 1:11) to judge the sinner and take me, along with all of His children to be with Him in heaven. (John 5:28-29).

In conclusion, our ultimate goal is to provide a clear understanding of Biblical prophecy regarding second coming events or eschatology.[9] We wish to challenge each of those who read this book to study the Bible more in depth on those subjects addressed here and be able to then articulate the information to others in such a way as to create a discussion about our Lord and Savior and His soon return. It is critically important and relevant in the times of crises we are living in today. It is our desire to help the Christian correctly understand Biblical prophecy. It can also be used in a small group or a Sunday School setting.

---

[9] See Glossary for definition of "Eschatology"

SECTION ONE

CHAPTER 1

IS A RAPTURE OF THE CHURCH INDICATED IN THE BIBLE

As we have now passed the 2,000[th] anniversary of Christ's first advent or coming, it seems there is a notable upsurge of interest in His second advent, as well as the whole subject of Bible prophecy. Until the late 20th century, this topic was one which was seldom discussed in the pulpits of the western world. Now it has become one of the hottest topics for religious speakers and writers. In 1970 author Hal Lindsey wrote a best-selling book entitled *"The Late Great Planet Earth"*. In the last few years, Tim LaHaye has topped the religious best-seller lists with a series of novels he has written centering on the Great Tribulation and the Second Coming of Jesus Christ to the earth. Prominent in the prophetic scenarios of Hal Lindsey, Tim LaHaye, and other Protestant evangelicals have been their teaching about the secret rapture of the church. All of the increased emphasis given to Bible prophecy in recent years has drawn much attention to the subject of the rapture. Perhaps you have even seen the bumper stickers on automobiles announcing that "In case of the rapture, this car will be without a driver!".

Most evangelicals who write or speak on the subject of prophecy assume the key end-time event for Christians is the secret rapture. What exactly is this secret rapture? What does the Bible teach concerning it, and is it the only hope for end-time Christians? There is a great deal of confusion about this and many aspects of prophecy in the professing Christian world. However, the real truth is both knowable and provable when we look to the plain, clear teachings of the Bible, rather than to the ideas and theories of men.

The Rapture Doctrine And Its Origin

What is the doctrine of the secret rapture? Simply put, it is the teaching that Jesus Christ will return twice! First, there will be a secret, unheralded return in which He will whisk all New Testament Christians, both living and dead, off to heaven to be present there during the time the "Great Tribulation" is taking place here on earth. This secret coming supposedly could occur at any moment and will come without any advance warning to anyone. Seven years later (or three and a half according to some) Christ will return openly in power and glory to destroy the wicked and to establish His Kingdom here on this earth for a thousand years.

It is interesting to note that the term "rapture" is used nowhere in the Bible. It is a term that has been invented by men and applied by them to what they term "the first phase" of the second coming. The Bible itself, however, nowhere says that Christ's coming will occur in phases. This is merely an assumption by the PTDs to try and support their view of the rapture.

The doctrine was promoted by John Nelson Darby beginning in the 1830s after an initial idea from a Catholic priest and later a vision by a lady in Darby's church. Darby was the founder of the Plymouth Brethren Church and developed a scheme of Scriptural interpretation called dispensationalism which included the rapture teaching. The idea of dispensationalists is that God has had different rules for different groups at different times. In fact, they teach that there are seven different dispensations.[10] God had the law for the Jews and now we have grace for the church. Granted, God gave the law for the Jews to follow, but it was still by faith that they followed God. The Jews were looking forward to a Messiah and we are looking back. Both follow God by faith. It is important to note that the dispensationalists have different ideas on when and how to apply the Word of God based on which dispensation they believe the Scripture fits into. In other words, they believe that only certain Scriptures apply to a specific dispensation. Sound confusing? It is. I have tried to discuss this with some dispensationalists and have found it to be very hard to see how the Bible is divided into seven separate and distinct periods of history. This will be addressed further

---

[10] See Glossary for explanation of seven dispensations

in the chapter titled "When Did the Church Begin".

This belief gained momentum when Darby's teachings were refined and popularized by C. I. Scofield, an American lawyer and minister who authored the noted Scofield Reference Bible at the beginning of the twentieth century. Primarily through Dr. C. I. Scofield, Protestant evangelicals came to generally accept the teachings of both dispensationalism PTDs and the secret rapture. These two ideas go hand in hand to confuse many sincere people as to God's real message for Christians as we near the end of time.

Proponents of the rapture point to I Thessalonians chapter 4 (see below) as their primary proof of a "secret coming". They then proceed to divide all Scriptures that discuss the return of Jesus Christ into two categories. First are the Scriptures that discuss the resurrection of the saints and their gathering to Christ. Second are the Scriptures that discuss Christ taking vengeance on wicked and rebellious people and nations. Their idea is that these events are separated by a period of years. They can do this only by assuming two separate comings. It's at this point that I wish to make a strong statement. Unless you first assume two separate comings, there is not one Scripture in the Bible that will support or indicate two comings.

One Coming Or Two?

Let's look at I Thessalonians chapter 4. Paul had preached and raised up a church in the Greek city of Thessalonica about AD50. Because of intense persecution, he was forced to leave the city and move on to other parts of Greece. While in Athens he sent his assistant Timothy back to Thessalonica bearing a letter intended to comfort and encourage the fledgling Christian community. In this context, he mentioned those who had already died in the faith. Since some were dead, how would they benefit from the return of the Messiah? Some in Thessalonica seem to have wondered. So Paul wrote the following to them:

I Thessalonians 4:13-17 (NIV)

[13]Brothers and sisters, we do not want you to be uninformed about those who sleep in death so that you do not grieve like the rest of mankind, who have no hope. [14]For we believe that Jesus died and rose again, and so we believe that God will bring with Jesus those who have fallen asleep in him. [15]According to the Lord's word, we tell you that we who are still alive, who are left until the coming of the Lord, will certainly not precede those who have fallen asleep.[16]For the Lord himself will come down from heaven, with a loud command, with the voice of the archangel and with the trumpet call of God, and the dead in Christ will rise first. [17]After that, we who are still alive and are left will be caught up together

with them in the clouds to meet the Lord in the air. And so we will be with the Lord forever.

This description is taken by rapture proponents to be the explanation and reason for a secret coming of Christ, which will take (rapture) Christians to heaven, and leave the unbelievers behind.[11] But notice, we are told, that preceding this resurrection the Lord will come with a loud command and the trumpet of God will be blown. How can a trumpet blow and a loud command happen if this is a secret coming?   The trumpet indicates an announcement of importance for all, not something in secret. The Apostle Paul added more details when he wrote a letter to the Corinthian Church, located in a neighboring Greek city.

Many teachers of a pre-tribulation rapture of the church use the following Scripture to support the rapture.

Luke 17:34-37 (NIV)

[34]*I tell you, on that night two people will be in one bed; one will be taken and the other left. *[35]*Two women will be grinding grain together; one will be taken and the other left* [36]*Two men will be in the field; one will be taken and the other left. *[37]*"Where, Lord?" they asked. He replied, "Where there is a dead body, there the vultures will gather."*

---

[11] See Glossary for explanation of "left behind"

It is interesting to note that not many of the PTD teachers use this Scripture anymore because it is obvious that Jesus is talking about where the dead bodies are taken. The disciples were not asking where is the one who is left. They already knew that. This passage supports the Lord's teaching in Matthew chapter 13 which shows the sinner is taken first. They are simply asking what happens to the one who is taken. I was puzzled by this initially since I heard this being taught as the rapture in my home church when I was a teenager. It was only after I discussed this with my father that he showed me the truth of what Jesus was teaching. He was the one who pointed out to me that the disciples were asking where the one was taken. The "where Lord" is simply asking about the one taken, not the one left behind. Do you honestly think that Jesus would describe His children as dead bodies being eaten by vultures?

I Corinthians 15:51-52 (NIV)

[51]*Listen, I tell you a mystery: We will not all sleep, but we will all be changed* [52]*in a flash, in the twinkling of an eye, at the last trumpet. For the trumpet will sound, the dead will be raised imperishable, and we will be changed.*

The specific supernatural trumpet that will be blown prior to the resurrection of the saints is dubbed "the last trumpet". So how many last trumpets are there? If there is more than one, there must be other trumpets that are not the "last trumpet". Does the Bible anywhere speak of a series of supernatural trumpet blasts? The answer is a resounding yes! Revelation 8:1-2 describes the opening of the seventh and last of the seals which had closed the book of Revelation until they were removed one at a time by Jesus Christ. When the seventh seal was opened, the Apostle John saw in vision seven angels standing before God and each receiving a trumpet. The angels proceeded to blow these trumpets one at a time signaling terrible ecological disasters followed by horrible warfare. Now, let us notice Revelation 11:15 and 18:

Revelation 11:15 & 18 (NIV)

15The seventh angel sounded his trumpet, and there were loud voices in heaven, which said: "The kingdom of the world has become the kingdom of our Lord and of his Messiah, and He will reign forever and ever."

18The nations were angry, and your wrath has come. The time has come for judging the dead, and for rewarding your servants the prophets and your people who revere your name, both great and small and for destroying those who destroy the earth."

Verse 18 connects this seventh and final trumpet blast with the time when God's wrath has come and when He would reward the saints. Clearly, when we look at these three sections of Scripture it is very apparent that the seventh and last trumpet signals both the resurrection of the saints as well as the time when Christ returns to judge the nations. These are not two different phases of the second coming, separated by seven years, as most evangelical writers contend.   Rather, the resurrection of the saints to immortality and the pouring out of God's wrath on the nations begin at the same time and are both signaled by the same event, the blast of the seventh and final trumpet.

The Parousia

The Bible uses the Greek word parousia numerous times to refer to the return of Jesus Christ. It is a term which was often used in a secular context to refer to the coming of a king. It carries with it no connotation of a secret coming. Four occurrences of the word are in Matthew 24.[12] In verse three Jesus' disciples asked Him for the "sign" of His parousia (or coming). In verse 27 Jesus compares His parousia to the visible spread of light from east to west when the sun rises. In verses 37 and 39 He compares His coming to the time when God's judgment came on the pre-flood world in the days of

---

[12] Matthew chapter 24 will be discussed in a separate chapter titled "Matthew Chapter 24 And The End Of The Age".

Noah. None of these verses are descriptive of any secret or clandestine coming. The word parousia is also used in I Corinthians 15:23 to refer to the event which will accompany the resurrection of the saints. In I Thessalonians 4:15 it is again used to refer to the event which accompanies the resurrection of the saints. Clearly His parousia will not be a secret event, but rather a time when He will begin to execute judgment on the ungodly.

Matthew 13:24-30 (NIV)

24Jesus told them another parable: "The kingdom of heaven is like a man who sowed good seed in his field. 25But while everyone was sleeping, his enemy came and sowed weeds among the wheat, and went away. 26When the wheat sprouted and formed heads, then the weeds also appeared.27"The owner's servants came to him and said, 'Sir, didn't you sow good seed in your field? Where then did the weeds come from?' 28"'An enemy did this,' he replied. "The servants asked him, 'Do you want us to go and pull them up?' 29"'No,' he answered, 'because while you are pulling the weeds, you may uproot the wheat with them. 30Let both grow together until the harvest. At that time I will tell the harvesters: First collect the weeds and tie them in bundles to be burned; then gather the wheat and bring it into my barn.'"

We need to use caution when using a parable to teach doctrine, but in this case, the Lord explains the parable in verses 37-43.

Matthew 13:37-43 (NIV)

37He answered, "The one who sowed the good seed is the Son of Man. 38The field is the world, and the good seed stands for the people of the kingdom. The weeds are the people of the evil one, 39and the enemy who sows them is the devil. The harvest is the end of the age, and the harvesters are angels. 40"As the weeds are pulled up and burned in the fire, so it will be at the end of the age. 41The Son of Man will send out his angels, and they will weed out of his kingdom everything that causes sin and all who do evil. 42They will throw them into the blazing furnace, where there will be weeping and gnashing of teeth. 43Then the righteous will shine like the sun in the kingdom of their Father. Whoever has ears, let them hear.

It cannot be any plainer than this passage of Scripture to show that there is no lifting out or rapture of the church with the sinners left behind. God's Word is clear.

The Last Day

Let's now take a look at what the Word of God says about when the resurrection will take place.

12

Understanding the teaching of PTDs regarding the Christians (church) being lifted out (raptured) prior to the tribulation, we must see if the Scriptures support or contradict that teaching.

Lazarus had just died and Jesus was talking to Martha about what was going to happen to him.

John 11:23-24 (NIV)

²³Jesus said to her, "Your brother will rise again." ²⁴Martha answered, "I know he will rise again in the resurrection at the last day."

If Martha was wrong regarding when Lazarus would be resurrected, this would have been the perfect time for Jesus to correct her. He would not have allowed her to be mistaken, but would have let her know that Lazarus would be lifted out (raptured) prior to the tribulation. Not only did Jesus not correct her, but He supported what she believed with statements of His own regarding "the last day". Let's look at some of them.

John 6:39-40 (NIV)

³⁹And this is the will of him who sent me, that I shall lose none of all those he has given me, but raise them up at the last day. ⁴⁰For my Father's will is that everyone who looks to the Son and believes in him shall have eternal life, and I will raise them up at the last day."

John 6:44 (NIV)

44 "No one can come to me unless the Father who sent me draws them, and I will raise them up at the last day.

John 6:54 (NIV)

54 Whoever eats my flesh and drinks my blood has eternal life, and I will raise them up at the last day.

The Greek word used in each of these verses for **last** is "eschatos" and it literally means final, end of, last, etc. The Greek word for **day** used in these verses is "hemera" and literally means the time between dawn and dark or a period of 24 hours. It is singular and cannot be understood as a period of time exceeding 24 hours. If it were plural, "the last days", then it could mean an indefinite period of time exceeding 24 hours. This phrase cannot be made any clearer. If God were to make it any plainer, what phrase could He use? Not only that, but Jesus continued to use the exact same phrase in teaching about what is to happen on "the last day".

In the above cases, Jesus is talking about His followers. Let's look at what He says about the lost.

John 12:48 (NIV)

⁴⁸There is a judge for the one who rejects me and does not accept my words; the very words I have spoken will condemn them at the last day.

Again, the last day used here, in the Greek, is "eschatos hemera" which means exactly what it says. If LaHaye and his followers are as literal as they claimed to be, then this should clear up any misunderstanding about rapture or lifting out of the church and leaving the sinner behind. Jesus used the same "last day" for the judgment of the sinner as He did when He was talking about the believers. They are all raised up and judged on "the last day".

There are no days after the last one. There can only be one "last day". I know this sounds simplistic, but it is important to understand there is no room for any other day after the last day. All other days are prior to the last day and therefore cannot be understood as another last day. The teaching of the pre-tribulation dispensationalists (PTDS) of two distinct and separate resurrections is obviously in error. The only way to believe what they teach is to ignore such passages as the ones above. These Scriptures clearly support John 5:28, 29, as well as the parable in Matthew chapter 13, which show only one resurrection of the dead where both the believer and the non-believer are resurrected at the same time. There simply is no room to insert an imaginary secret rapture of the saints in these passages as well as in many others. You may continue to believe in two separate comings, but you must know that there are no Scriptures to support it.

God Is Consistent

The PTDs teach that God will rapture His church from this earth to save them from the "Great Tribulation" that is to follow the rapture. The following events should help us understand how God protects His people. Let's look first at the worldwide flood and see how God kept Noah and his family.

Noah And The Ark

In Genesis chapters 6-8, we see God protecting Noah and his family during the most catastrophic event that ever took place on this earth. God did not rapture or lift Noah and his family out of this world. Just as the Lord promised to protect (tereo)[13] His followers in Rev. 3:10, He protected Noah, here on this earth, not somewhere else. This should be a good word picture for us in that God will be with us no matter what we are going through.

_____

[13] See glossary for definition of tereo

Daniel In The Lion's Den

Daniel 6:16 (NIV)

[16]So the king gave the order, and they brought Daniel and threw him into the lions' den. The king said to Daniel, "May your God, whom you serve continually, rescue you!"

Daniel was put in the lion's den because he refused to worship King Darius. King Darius did not want to put Daniel in the lion's den. This decree was put in place to find fault with Daniel because the leaders could find no reason to remove him from his position of authority otherwise. Please read the entire 6th chapter of the book of Daniel to understand the complete story. Now let's see how God protected Daniel.

Daniel 6:22 (NIV)

[22]My God sent his angel, and he shut the mouths of the lions. They have not hurt me, because I was found innocent in his sight. Nor have I ever done any wrong before you, Your Majesty."

It is important we realize the way God works. He did not lift Daniel out of the lion's den. God protected Daniel in the den by shutting the mouths of the lions. He could have raptured Daniel out of the den, but instead showed His power of protection by leaving Daniel where he was and keeping him safe.

Shadrach, Meshach, & Abednego

Here is an overview of what happened in the book of Daniel chapter 3, but you need to read the entire chapter. We have the account of King Nebuchadnezzar issuing an order for everyone in his kingdom to fall down and worship the image he had made. The three Hebrew children refused to worship the image and as a result were thrown into a fiery furnace which was fired seven times hotter than normal. When the three were put into the furnace, it was so hot that it killed the men who threw them into the furnace. When the king went to check on the status of the three men, he was astonished.

Daniel 3:24-25 (NIV)

[24]Then King Nebuchadnezzar leaped to his feet in amazement and asked his advisers, "Weren't there three men that we tied up and threw into the fire?" They replied, "Certainly, Your Majesty." [25]He said, "Look! I see four men walking around in the fire, unbound and unharmed, and the fourth looks like the Son of the God."

Not only did God protect the three, but He walked with them in the midst of the fire. Isn't that just like our Lord? When we are in trouble, He will be with us through it. It should be understood there will be various ways of how God goes about His protection for us. We know there will be times of trial and testing and also we may be called on to give our life for the Gospel. As an example, all of the disciples except John were martyred for their commitment to spreading the message of salvation. So we don't know if God will supernaturally protect us, as in the examples above, or if we will be called upon to give our life for His message. It really doesn't matter. Either way He is with us.

Conclusion

1. There are no Scriptures that indicate two separate comings of the Lord. The Bible clearly shows that the Lord's coming will be visible and one time only.
2. Until Darby taught this idea in the 1830s, the church believed in only one coming.
3. Is the loud voice and the trumpet mentioned in I Thessalonians chapter 4 silent?
4. Why aren't the "left behind" sinners mentioned in I Thessalonians chapter 4?
5. The parable of the sower in Matthew chapter 13 clearly shows that the good and the bad will grow together until the harvest.
6. Notice who is taken first in the explanation of the parable in Matthew chapter 13.
7. Notice that Jesus deals with the good and bad seed at the end.
8. Does John 5:28-29 leave the sinner behind and the Christian raptured?
9. Does Luke chapter 17:34-37 clear up any misunderstandings regarding the rapture?
10. Are there any days left after the "last day"?

CHAPTER 2

DANIEL'S 70TH WEEK

The second leg of the milk stool is the teaching by dispensationalists that there will be a seven-year period of tribulation[14] upon the earth immediately after the Christians have been lifted out or raptured by the Lord.

A lie can travel halfway around the world while the truth is still putting on its shoes. — Mark Twain (1835-1910)

I would like to modify that a little by saying that a false doctrine can travel all over the world while the truth is still putting on its shoes. I believe this statement can truly be said regarding a last-days tribulation period consisting of seven years.

I trust after you read this chapter you will see the importance of comprehending this passage and how it relates to last-days prophecy.

In chapter one, we have addressed the fact that there is no rapture or "lifting out" of the church prior to the visible return of Christ. The idea of a seven-year tribulation period on this earth which follows a secret coming of Christ is also a false teaching of the PTDs that we must address.

The debate about whether Jesus Christ will

---

[14] See Glossary for explanation of "The Great Tribulation"

return for His church before, during or after the seven years of tribulation seems to be the topic of the day, when by far the most important question worth asking is: Does the Bible really predict a future "seven-year period of tribulation" at all? Is this just something that is being taught without Biblical support or someone's idea that seems to fit with an overall concept that cannot be justified by the Word of God?

Here is a bold statement that hopefully will get your attention. There is no specific Bible text predicting any seven-year tribulation. Let me repeat that. There is not one Scripture anywhere in the Bible that will support a seven-year tribulation without first making a lot of assumptions. The entire concept is based on a false interpretation of one primary verse, even though it is a popular teaching in many of our churches today.

Virtually all theologians agree that the 70 weeks found in Daniel 9:24 equates literally to 490 years. Each day of the 70 weeks represents a literal one year period (70 weeks X 7 days = 490 years). Therefore, the 70th week represents the last seven-year period found in Daniel's prophecy.

Daniel 9:24-27 (NIV)

24 "Seventy 'sevens' are decreed for your people and your holy city to finish transgression, to put an end to sin, to atone for wickedness, to bring in everlasting righteousness, to seal up vision and prophecy and to anoint the Most Holy Place. 25 "Know and understand this: From the time the word goes out to restore and rebuild Jerusalem until the Anointed One, the ruler, comes, there will be seven 'sevens,' and sixty-two 'sevens.' It will be rebuilt with streets and a trench but in times of trouble. 26 After the sixty-two 'sevens,' the Anointed One will be put to death and will have nothing. The people of the ruler who comes will destroy the city and the sanctuary. The end will come like a flood: War will continue until the end, and desolations have been decreed. 27 He will confirm a covenant with many for one seven. In the middle of the 'seven', He will put an end to sacrifice and offering. And at the temple, he will set up an abomination that causes desolation until the end that is decreed is poured out on him.

Dispensationalists often conclude the following from verse 27:

1. "He" is the antichrist.

2. Antichrist will make a covenant with the Jews for "one week" (the last "week" of the 70-week/490-year prophecy)–meaning seven years of tribulation.

3. In the middle of the seven-year tribulation, the antichrist will cause the sacrifices of a rebuilt Jewish temple "to cease".

The Dispensationalists teach Daniel 9:27 is applied to antichrist (point 1), a seven-year tribulation (point 2), and a rebuilt Jewish temple (point 3). The verse itself doesn't say anything about any of this. This is merely an assumption on their part to place Daniel's prophecy sequentially after the church has been raptured and before the Lord returns for His millennial (1000-year) reign. The fact is that many, if not most, credible Bible scholars of the past have applied Daniel 9:27 to Jesus Christ, not the antichrist. Several credible commentaries also do not agree with a seven-year tribulation period that is in the future. Also, there are no Scriptures indicating a rebuilt temple.

Listed below are just three of the many solid commentaries that do not support the idea that Daniel's writing is referring to a future antichrist.

Matthew Henry's commentary on Daniel 9:27 states, "By offering himself a sacrifice once and for all, He [Jesus], shall put an end to all the Levitical sacrifices."

Adam Clarke's commentary says during Daniel 9:27's "term of seven years", Jesus Himself would "confirm or ratify the new covenant with mankind".

The **Jamieson, Fausset, and Brown** commentary also says: "He shall confirm the covenant—Christ. The confirmation of the covenant is assigned to Him."

Here are some points that provide solid evidence that Daniel's 70th week doesn't refer to any future tribulation at all. Rather, it was fulfilled nearly two thousand years ago.

1. The prophecy of "seventy weeks" means seventy straight sequential weeks. There is no example in Scripture (or anywhere else) of a time period starting, stopping, and then starting again. This idea of a long period of time between the 69th and 70th weeks of Daniel is only done to support an idea that there is a seven-year period of tribulation yet to come. The gap has only been inserted by the dispensationalists to support their belief of a seven-year tribulation period after the church has been lifted out (raptured). It simply isn't true, but a mere assumption on their part.

2. The 70th week follows immediately after the 69th week. If it doesn't, then it cannot properly be called the 70th week.

3. It makes no sense to insert a 2,000-year or more gap between the 69th and 70th weeks. There is no gap between the first seven weeks and sixty-two weeks. Why insert one between the 69th and 70th weeks? To me, this is a terrible misapplication of God's Word. If we can insert an unmentioned belief in this passage, then we should be

able to insert what we believe whenever and wherever we want to.

4. Daniel 9:27 says nothing about any "tribulation", "rebuilt" Jewish temple, or "antichrist". Again, this is merely an assumption without any support. We can build any doctrinal application we want if we merely assume something, whether it be true to the Word or not.

5. Daniel 9:24-27's focus is on the Messiah. After the Messiah is "cut off" (referring to Christ's death), "the people of the prince who is to come shall destroy the city and the sanctuary". This refers to the destruction of Jerusalem by Roman armies led by Prince Titus in AD70. We will deal more with the destruction of Jerusalem later.

6. "He shall confirm the covenant." Paul said "the covenant" was "confirmed before by God in Christ" (Galatians 3:17). Jesus Christ came "to confirm the promises made to the fathers" (Romans 15:8). The word "covenant" is Messianic and always applies to the Messiah, never to an antichrist.

7. "He shall confirm the covenant with many." Jesus said, "This is my blood of the new covenant, which is shed for many..." (Matthew 26:28). Jesus was quoting Daniel 9:27 specifically.

8. "In the midst of the week, he shall cause the sacrifice to cease." After 3 ½ years of ministry, Jesus Christ's death put an end to all sacrifices in God's sight. He is the Final Sacrifice! Please read Hebrews chapter 10.

9. It was abominable for the Jewish leaders to put God's Son to death. This ended their need for a sacrifice in the temple which was destroyed in AD70. Jesus predicted, "Your house is left to you desolate" (Matthew 23:38).

10. The 70 weeks applied to the Jewish people (Daniel 9:24). Christ's public ministry lasted 3 ½ years during which His focus was "the lost sheep of the house of Israel" (Matthew 10:6). After His resurrection and then for another 3 ½ years, His disciples preached mostly to Jews (see Acts 1-6). When the Jewish Sanhedrin stoned Stephen in AD34 (see Acts 7), the Gospel focus shifted to the Gentiles (see Acts 13:46)—exactly as prophecy predicted, which ended the 70th week. This ended the ministry that was directed specifically at the Jewish nation. There is no gap between the 69th and 70th weeks recorded in Daniel or anywhere else for that matter.

The truth is overwhelming! These eight words found in Daniel 9:27: "**confirm... covenant... many... midst... sacrifice... cease... abominations... desolate**" all find perfect fulfillment in Jesus Christ and early Christian history. One major reason why the Jewish nation as a whole failed to receive its Messiah was because its scholars misinterpreted Daniel 9:27. They failed to see Jesus Christ as the predicted One who would die in the midst of the 70th week! The same thing is happening today as some Christian scholars misapply the same prophecy. Isn't it interesting that the Jews and the dispensationalists have both missed the "right in your face" prophecy in Daniel that applies to the Messiah?

The future "seven-year tribulation theory" is just that, a theory without support. When Daniel 9:24-27 is correctly understood, there is no seven-year period yet to come. It is not in our future because it has already happened as will be seen in our next chapter called "The Great Tribulation". There is no Bible text that teaches any "seven-year tribulation". It cannot be found, only assumed, which is what much of the dispensationalists' teaching is, only an assumption.

Jesus Christ confirmed the covenant and caused the sacrifices "to cease". The covenant was made by Jesus and He alone is the final sacrifice and only He can make a covenant.

When Did The 70 Weeks Begin?

It is not absolutely necessary to understand when the 70 weeks began, but more of an idea to help clarify and establish the prophecy recorded by Daniel. When did the 70 weeks (or actually 490 years) that are prophesied in Daniel chapter 9 start? After much study, I have concluded that it started in 457BC based on the edict of the king to rebuild Jerusalem. (See the chart at the end of this chapter.) It is accepted by virtually all scholars that the first 69 weeks are consecutive. The end of the 69th week would then be AD27 when Jesus was baptized and began His public ministry. Counting 3 ½ years from that time would take us to the Lord's crucifixion which is the middle of the 70th week. The final 3 ½ years of the 70th week was the effort to evangelize the Jewish people and ended in AD34 with the stoning of Stephen. It was at that time the ministry of the disciples began to focus on the Gentiles. Daniel's prophetic 70 weeks (490 years) was fulfilled.

This chart depicts Daniel's70 weeks copied from preteristarchive.com/ARTchive/Charts.

490 YEARS

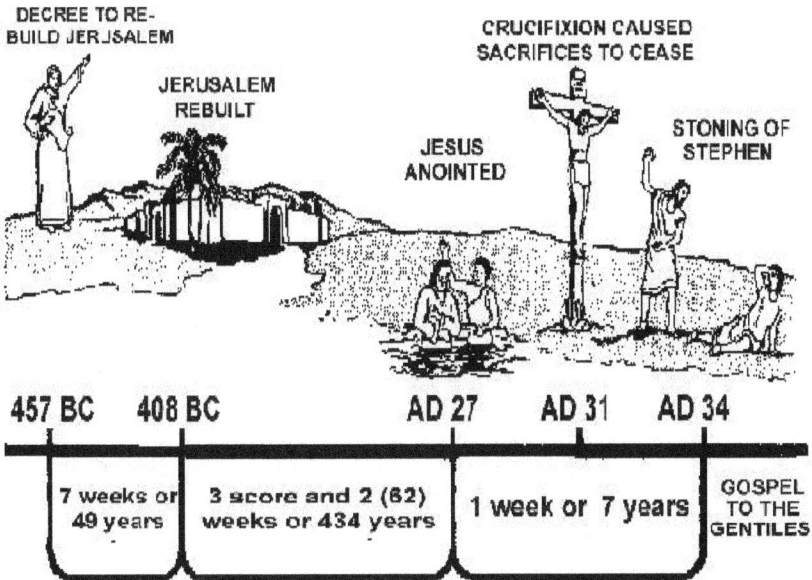

| DECREE TO RE-BUILD JERUSALEM | JERUSALEM REBUILT | JESUS ANOINTED | CRUCIFIXION CAUSED SACRIFICES TO CEASE | STONING OF STEPHEN |

457 BC	408 BC		AD 27	AD 31	AD 34
7 weeks or 49 years	3 score and 2 (62) weeks or 434 years		1 week or 7 years		GOSPEL TO THE GENTILES

Conclusion

1. Is the "He" in Daniel chapter 9 the antichrist or Jesus?

2. Can anyone make a covenant besides the Lord?

3. In the middle of the 70th week, what or who causes the sacrifices to cease?

4. If there is no gap between the first 7 weeks and the next 62 weeks of Daniel, then why is there a gap between the 69th and 70th week?

CHAPTER 3

THE GREAT TRIBULATION

Matthew 24:21 **(NIV)**

²¹*For then there will be great distress, unequaled from the beginning of the world until now and never to be equaled again.*

We have chopped the second leg out from under the milk stool by having looked at the fact that there is no future seven-year period of great tribulation in our last chapter and no gap between the 69th and 70th weeks of Daniel. Let's look at when and what did happen during the period of time that Jesus is teaching about in this passage.

This is a long chapter with many quotes from the Jewish historian Josephus but I felt that it was important to include some of his writings for clarity. I make no apology for repeating the central theme being taught by the pre-tribulation dispensationalists or PTDs. It is critical that you understand clearly what they are teaching and how non-biblical it is.

Very few Christians alive, if any, have not heard of the "Great Tribulation". It is supposed to be a future terrible time on earth that will affect all of those who are alive. Christians and even non-Christians have heard several sermons about it, read books about it, and even seen movies about it. PTDs teach that someday soon Christ will return to the earth invisibly and rapture away all the Christians or there will be a secret lifting out of the church. After God has removed the church, He will go back to dealing with Israel. They teach there will be a terrible seven-year period called the tribulation in which the earth and its inhabitants will be overwhelmed by God's wrath. Among the dispensationalists, there are those who hold different positions as to when the rapture will happen. Some believe the rapture will happen before the start of a seven-year tribulation period, some believe it will happen halfway through the seven-year tribulation period and some believe it will happen at the end of the seven-year tribulation period. They may have different opinions on when the rapture takes place, but all teach a secret rapture or lifting out of the church. Then at the end of this future seven-year tribulation period, Christ will return with His saints and begin a millennial or thousand year reign on this earth. At the end of the 1000-years there will be a rebellion, as Satan has been loosed for a season, but Christ will destroy the rebels and the eternal state will begin. I have read literally dozens of opinions presented by the PTDs and can find no majority that agree on exactly how this is all supposed to happen. It is honestly one of the most confusing approaches to eschatology regarding the millennium or thousand years that I have ever seen. The more I study the PTDs' belief on this, the more I am convinced that even they don't know what they believe. I will try to address some of the questions about this confusion in the chapter titled "The Thousand Years".

The entire scheme of dispensational eschatology or second coming prophecy, though popular in recent years, has no roots in historic Christian interpretation of the Scriptures. After studying Revelation, I believe that the "Great Tribulation" was the destruction of Jerusalem by the Roman army from AD67 to AD70. This had been the most accepted belief of Christians throughout the history of the church until the last hundred and eighty years or so when the dispensationalists have placed the tribulation at some future time.

When Was The Great Tribulation?

Is the "Great Tribulation" something that is yet to come or is it a past event? Is Matthew 24 also talking about a time in the future or something that happened in the time of the disciples? After reading and studying several books and Biblical passages on this event, it has become abundantly clear to me that this has already happened. It happened in the first century. I must confess to you that until recent years, I too believed there would be a future time of great tribulation and that it would signal the visible return of Christ. This is not to say a terrible time couldn't come upon the earth in the future, but the Biblical account does not indicate that. In fact, I will address this later on the world's troubles as we approach the end of time.

In Matthew 24 Jesus is answering the disciples' questions about the destruction of Jerusalem. They wanted to know when it would be destroyed, and what signs would precede the end of the age and His parousia. After talking about the abomination of desolation, which was when Jerusalem was surrounded by armies and what happened later during the siege, Jesus talks about the "Great Tribulation".

Matthew 24:15-21 (NIV)

[15]*"So when you see standing in the holy place 'the abomination that causes desolation,' spoken of through the prophet Daniel—let the reader understand—* [16]*then let those who are in Judea flee to the mountains.* [17]*Let no one on the housetop go down to take anything out of the house.* [18]*Let no one in the field go back to get their cloak.* [19]*How dreadful it will be in those days for pregnant women and nursing mothers!* [20]*Pray that your flight will not take place in winter or on the Sabbath* [21]*For then there will be great distress, unequaled from the beginning of the world until now—and never to be equaled again."*

"Then" is when? Within a few thousand years? The "then" is referring to the context of verses 15-20 when you see the abomination of desolation, which Luke tells us is Jerusalem surrounded by armies. This happened in

AD67 when Cestius Gallus, the Roman general, invaded Jerusalem. The Great Tribulation is not an event which is yet to come. It was "then", during the siege of Jerusalem by the Romans in the first century. This is made abundantly clear in the parallel text in Luke's Gospel.

Luke 21:20-24 (NIV)

[20]*"When you see Jerusalem being surrounded by armies, you will know that its desolation is near.* [21]*Then let those who are in Judea flee to the mountains, let those in the city get out, and let those in the country not enter the city.* [22]*For this is the time of punishment in fulfillment of all that has been written.* [23]*How dreadful it will be in those days for pregnant women and nursing mothers! There will be great distress in the land and wrath against this people.* [24]*They will fall by the sword and will be taken as prisoners to all the nations. Jerusalem will be trampled on by the Gentiles until the times of the Gentiles are fulfilled.*

Luke tells us here that **ALL** things which are written will be fulfilled in the destruction of Jerusalem. What does he mean by that? All things which are written refers to prophecy. All prophecy was to be fulfilled in the destruction of Jerusalem. Daniel tells us this very same thing in Daniel 9:24.

Notice the "who" in Luke 21:23 says the tribulation will come upon "the land", which is Jerusalem and "this people". This is referring to the first century Jews, not some future inclusion of the whole world. Verse 24 then gives us added details as to exactly what will, or did, happen in the Great Tribulation.

Daniel's prophecy tells of the time when all prophecy would cease to be given and what had been given would be fulfilled. When would this be? Daniel's vision ends with the destruction of Jerusalem which we know occurred in AD70.

Daniel 9:26 (NIV)

[26]*After the sixty two 'sevens,' the Anointed One will be put to death and will have nothing. The people of the ruler who comes will destroy the city and the sanctuary. The end will come like a flood: War will continue until the end, and desolations have been decreed.*

William Kimball[15], in his book, *What the Bible Says About the Great Tribulation* said, "This period of great tribulation is not an event which the entire world is yet awaiting, but a past historic event of unparalleled concentrated severity specifically afflicting the Jewish nation in AD70."

Eusebius of Caesarea[16], who lived in the third

---

[15] William R. Kimball, president of "Disciples Indeed" Bible School in South Lake Tahoe, California

[16]*Eusébios*; AD 260/265 – 339/340), also known as **Eusebius Pamphili**, was a Roman historian, and Christian polemicist of Greek descent. He became the bishop of Caesarea Maritima about 314.

century said he believed that "the flight of the Christians, the abomination of desolation, and the great tribulation, were all connected with the events leading up to the destruction of Jerusalem in AD70."

John Walvoord[17], a leading spokesman for dispensationalism, says this: "The great tribulation, is a specific period of time beginning with the abomination of desolation[18] and it closes with the second coming of Christ, in the light of Daniel's prophecies and confirmed by reference to forty-two months. In Revelation 11:2 and 13:5, the great tribulation is a specific three-and-a-half-year period leading up to the second coming."[19] Now, Walvoord sees all of these things as yet future, but if we can establish that the abomination of desolation and the Great Tribulation are passed, then Walvoord is incorrect in his timing.

Let's look at what exactly happened in AD67 to AD70 and see if it truly was "the Great Tribulation" and "the days of vengeance". Because most Christians are

---

Together with Pamphilus, he was a scholar of the Biblical canon and is regarded as an extremely well learned Christian of his time.

[17] **John F. Walvoord** (May 1, 1910 – December 20, 2002) was a Christian theologian, pastor, and president of Dallas Theological Seminary from 1952 to 1986. He was the author of over 30 books, focusing primarily on eschatology and theology including *The Rapture Question*.

[18] We saw this began in AD67 when Cestius Gallus, the Roman general, laid siege to Jerusalem.

[19] Copied from Ecclesia.org, David B. Curtis titled: The Great Tribulation

totally unfamiliar with the events of this 42 month period, they can't understand how it was the Great Tribulation. The Bible only predicts the events of Jerusalem's fall because none of the prophecies in the Bible were spoken about after AD70; so to find out what happened at that time, we need to look at history.

Most of the history that we are going to look at comes from Josephus[20], a Jewish historian, who lived and wrote at the time of Jerusalem's destruction. The first two quotes from Josephus comes from the preface to "The Wars of the Jews". The balance of his quotes in this chapter is from his book. I have included many of Josephus' writings from the book as proof of the total destruction of Jerusalem. Granted, some of Josephus' writings included here are lengthy but to get a real idea of what happened during the siege of Jerusalem, it is important to read about the utter devastation that took place at that time.

Josephus Said This:

"Whereas the war which the Jews made with the Romans hath been the greatest of all those, not only that have been in our times, but, in a manner, of those that were ever heard of." (PREFACE, Section 1)

Josephus, <u>who was not a Christian</u>, agrees with

---

[20]Josephus' writings are regarded as the most accurate historical record of what happened to the Jews during the first century. His detailed account is taught in many colleges and seminaries.

Jesus' words in Matthew 24:21, that the war with the Romans was "the greatest of all wars ever heard of". What was it that caused this war? Many think the Romans just decided to crush the Jews, so they destroyed Jerusalem. This is not the case. Rome did not initiate the war against Jerusalem. The zealots in Jerusalem had incited the Jews to rebel against Rome.

Josephus Further Said This:

"However, I will not go to the other extreme, out of opposition to those men who extol the Romans, nor will I determine to raise the actions of my countrymen too high; but I will prosecute the actions of both parties with accuracy. Yet I shall suit my language to the passions I am under, as to the affairs I describe, and must be allowed to indulge some lamentation upon the miseries undergone by my own country; for that it was a seditious temper of our own that destroyed it; and that they were the tyrants among the Jews who brought the Roman power upon us, who unwillingly attacked us, and occasioned the burning of our holy temple; Titus Caesar, who destroyed it, is himself a witness, who, during the entire war, pitied the people who were kept under by the seditious, and did often voluntarily delay the taking of the city, and allowed time to the siege, in order to let the authors have opportunity for repentance. Accordingly it appears to me, that the misfortunes of all men, from the beginning of the world if they are compared to these of the Jews, are not so considerable as they were; while the

authors of them were not foreigners neither."Preface, Section 4

The Jews also rebelled by ceasing to offer a sacrifice for Caesar. Josephus says this was the beginning of the war. The city was full of wickedness and the people appointed high priests of unknown and questionable persons who cooperated with them in their wickedness. Josephus records the regular high priest, Ananus, as saying, "Certainly, it had been good for me to die before I had seen the house of God full of so many abominations." The wickedness within the city was great, the city was in civil war. Josephus tells us what went on in the city.

Josephus Recorded The Following:

"And indeed many there were of the Jews that deserted every day, and fled away from the zealots, although their flight was very difficult, since they had guarded every passage out of the city, and slew everyone that was caught at them, as taking it for granted they were going over to the Romans; yet did he who gave them money get clear off, while he only that gave them none was voted a traitor. So the upshot was this, that the rich purchased their flight by money while none but the poor were slain. Along all the roads also vast numbers of dead bodies lay in heaps, and even many of those that were so zealous in deserting at length chose rather to perish within the city; for the hopes of burial made death in

their own city appear of the two less terrible to them. But these zealots came at last to that degree of barbarity, as not to bestow a burial either on those slain in the city, or on those that lay along the roads; but as if they had made an agreement to cancel both the laws of their country and the laws of nature, and, at the same time that they defiled men with their wicked actions, they would pollute the Divinity itself also, they left the dead bodies to putrefy under the sun; and the same punishment was allotted to such as buried any as to those that deserted, which was no other than death; while he that granted the favor of a grave to another would presently stand in need of a grave himself. To say all in a word, no other gentle passion was so entirely lost among them as mercy; for what were the greatest objects of pity did most of all irritate these wretches, and they transferred their rage from the living to those that had been slain, and from the dead to the living. Nay, the terror was so very great, that he who survived called them that were first dead happy, as being at rest already; as did those that were under torture in the prisons, declare, that, upon this comparison, those that lay unburied were the happiest. These men, therefore, trampled upon all the laws of men, and laughed at the laws of God; and for the oracles of the prophets, they ridiculed them as the tricks of jugglers; yet did these prophets foretell many things concerning [the rewards of] virtue, and [punishments of] vice, which when these zealots violated, they occasioned the fulfilling of those very prophecies belonging to their own country; for there was a certain ancient oracle of those men, that the city should then be taken and the sanctuary burnt, by right of war, when a sedition should invade the Jews, and their own hand should pollute the temple of God. Now while these zealots did not [quite] disbelieve these predictions, they made themselves the instruments of their accomplishment." (*Josephus Book IV, Chapter VI, Section 3*)

In light of what Josephus says here about the dead bodies lying in heaps and rotting in the sun, look at the prophecy in Amos 8:1-3.

Amos 8:1-3 (NIV)

[1]This is what the Sovereign LORD showed me: a basket of ripe fruit. [2]"What do you see, Amos?" he asked. "A basket of ripe fruit," I answered. Then the LORD said to me, "The time is ripe for my people Israel; I will spare them no longer". [3]"In that day," declares the Sovereign LORD, "the songs in the temple will turn to wailing. Many, many bodies—flung everywhere! Silence!"

Why was this happening to Israel? They had broken the covenant with their God. They had turned from God and thus were suffering a covenantal judgment.

The destruction of an immense quantity of corn and other provisions by the rebels was the direct occasion of a terrible famine, which consumed incredible numbers of Jews in Jerusalem during its siege.

More Of What Josephus Recorded:

"And now there were three treacherous factions in the city, the one parted from the other. Eleazar and his party, that kept the sacred first-fruits, came against John in their cups. Those that were with John plundered the populace and went out with zeal against Simon. This Simon had his supply of provisions from the city, in opposition to the seditious. When, therefore, John was assaulted on both sides, he made his men turn about, throwing his darts upon those citizens that came up against him, from the cloisters he had in his possession, while he opposed those that attacked him from the temple by engines of war; and if at any time he was freed from those that were above him, which happened frequently, from their being drunk and tired, he sallied out with a great number upon Simon and his party; and this he did always in such parts of the city as he could come at till he set on fire those houses that were full of corn, and of all provisions. The same thing was done by Simon, when, upon the others' retreat, he attacked the city also; as if they had, on purpose done it to serve the Romans, by destroying what the city had laid up against the Siege, and by thus cutting off the nerves of their own power. Accordingly, it so came to pass, that all the places that were about the temple were burnt down, and became an intermediate desert space, ready for

fighting on both sides; and that almost all the corn was burnt, which would have been sufficient for a siege of many years. So they were taken by the means of famine, which it was impossible they should have been unless they had thus prepared the way for it by this procedure."
(*Josephus Book V, Chapter I, Section 4*)

Josephus Records The Fulfillment Of These Awful Prophecies:

"And, indeed, why do I relate these particular calamities? while Manneus, the son of Lazarus, came running to Titus at this very time, and told him that there had been carried out through that one gate, which was entrusted to his care, no fewer than a hundred and fifteen thousand eight hundred and eighty dead bodies, in the interval between the fourteenth day of the month Xanthieus, [Nisan,] when the Romans pitched their camp by the city, and the first day of the month Panemus [Tamuz]. This was itself a prodigious multitude; and though this man was not himself set as a governor at that gate, yet was he appointed to pay the public stipend for carrying these bodies out, and so was obliged of necessity to number them, while the rest were buried by their relations; though all their burial was but this, to bring them away, and cast them out of the city. After this man there ran away to Titus many of the eminent citizens, and told him the entire number of the poor that were dead, and that no fewer than six hundred thousand

were thrown out at the gates, though still the number of the rest could not be discovered; and they told him further, that when they were no longer able to carry out the dead bodies of the poor, they laid their corpses on heaps in very large houses, and shut them up therein; as also that a medimnus of wheat was sold for a talent; and that when, a while afterward, it was not possible to gather herbs, by reason the city was all walled about, some persons were driven to that terrible distress as to search the common sewers and old dunghills of cattle, and to eat the dung which they got there; and what they of old could not endure so much as to see they now used for food. When the Romans barely heard all this, they commiserated their case; while the seditious, who saw it also, did not repent, but suffered the same distress to come upon themselves; for they were blinded by that fate which was already coming upon the city, and upon themselves also."(Josephus BookV Chapter XIII Section 7)

The depth of this famine is clearly seen in the gut-wrenching story that Josephus tells of Mary.

"Now there was a certain woman that dwelt beyond Jordan, her name was Mary; her father was Eleazar, of the village Bethezub, which signifies the House of Hyssop. She was eminent for her family and her wealth, and had fled away to Jerusalem with the rest of the multitude, and was with them besieged therein at this time. The other effects of this woman had been already seized upon; such I mean as she had brought with her

out of Perea, and removed to the city. What she had treasured up beside, as also what food she had contrived to save, had also been carried off by the rapacious guards, who came every day running into her house for that purpose. This put the poor woman into a very great passion, and by the frequent reproaches and imprecations she cast at these rapacious villains, she had provoked them to anger against her; but none of them, either out of the indignation she had raised against herself, or out of the commiseration of her case, would take away her life; and if she found any food, she perceived her labors were for others, and not for herself; and it was now become impossible for her anyway to find any more food, while the famine pierced through her very bowels and marrow, when also her passion was fired to a degree beyond the famine itself: nor did she consult with anything but with her passion and the necessity she was in. She then attempted a most unnatural thing; and snatching up her son, who was a child sucking at her breast, she said, 'O thou miserable infant! for whom shall I preserve thee in this war, this famine, and this sedition? As to the war with the Romans, if they preserve our lives, we must be slaves! The famine also will destroy us, even before that slavery comes upon us; yet are these seditious rogues more terrible than both the other. Come on; be thou my food, and be thou a fury to these seditious varlets and a byword to the world, which is all that is now wanting to complete the calamities of us Jews.' As soon as she had *said this, she slew her son; and then roasted him, and ate one-half of him, and kept the other half by her concealed. Upon this the seditious come in presently, and smelling the horrid scent of this food, they threatened her that they would cut her throat immediately if she did not shew them what food she had gotten ready. She replied, that she had saved a very fine portion of it for them; and withal uncovered what was left of her son. Hereupon they were seized with a horror and amazement of mind, and stood astonished at the sight; when she said to them 'This is mine own son; and what hath been done was mine own doing! Come, eat of this food; for I have eaten of it myself! Do not you pretend to be either more tender than a woman, or more compassionate than a mother; but if you be so scrupulous, and do abominate this my sacrifice, as I have eaten the one-half, let the rest be reserved for me also.' After which, those men went out trembling, being never so much affrighted at anything as they were at this, and with some difficulty they left the rest of that meat to the mother. Upon which, the whole city was full of horrid action immediately; and while everyone laid this miserable case before their own eyes, they trembled, as if this unheard-of-action had been done by themselves. So those that were thus distressed by the famine were very desirous to die, and those already dead were esteemed happy because they had not lived long enough either to hear or see such miseries."* (*Josephus Book VI, Chapter III, Section 4*)

Let's look at Deuteronomy 28:53 & 57 and see the awfulness that is being predicted here. Recorded above is Josephus' historic account of how they ate their own children.

Deuteronomy 28:53 (NIV)

53Because of the suffering, your enemy will inflict on you during the siege, you will eat the fruit of the womb, the flesh of the sons and daughters the LORD your God has given you.

Deuteronomy 28:57 (NIV)

57the afterbirth from her womb and the children she bears. For in her dire need, she intends to eat them secretly because of the suffering your enemy will inflict on you during the siege of your cities.

I would strongly encourage you to read Deuteronomy 28 in its entirety, keeping in mind what we have presented here. I hope that by now you are beginning to understand the words of Jesus.

Matthew 24:21 (NIV)

21For then there will be great distress, unequaled from the beginning of the world until now—and never to be equaled again.

Just One More Thing From Josephus:

"Hereupon some of the deserters, having no other way, leaped down from the wall immediately, while others of them went out of the city with stones, as if they would fight them; but thereupon they fled away to the Romans. But here a worse fate accompanied these than what they had found within the city; and they met with a quicker dispatch from the too great abundance they had among the Romans, than they could have done from the famine among the Jews; for when they came first to the Romans, they were puffed up by the famine, and swelled like men in a dropsy; after which they all on the sudden overfilled those bodies that were before empty, and so burst asunder, excepting such only as were skillful enough to restrain their appetites, and by degrees took in their food into bodies unaccustomed thereto. Yet did another plague seize upon those that were thus preserved; for there was found among the Syrian deserters a certain person who was caught gathering pieces of gold out of the excrements of the Jews' bellies; for the deserters used to swallow such pieces of gold, as we told you before, when they came out, and for these did the seditious search them all; for there was a great quantity of gold in the city, insomuch that as much was now sold [in the Roman camp] for twelve Attic [drams], as was sold before for twenty-five. But when this contrivance was discovered in one instance, the fame of it filled their several camps, that

the deserters came to them full of gold. So the multitude of the Arabians, with the Syrians, cut up those that came as supplicants and searched their bellies. Nor does it seem to me that any misery befell the Jews that was more terrible than this since in one night's time about two thousand of these deserters were thus dissected."(Josephus Book V, Chapter XIII, Section 4)

Israel had crucified the Lord and publicly called God's judgment down on themselves: And all the people answered and said this in Matthew 27:25.

Matthew 27:25 (NIV)

25All the people answered, "His blood is on us and on our children!"

God's judgment on Israel in AD70 matched their crime, the crucifixion of Christ. This crime was the worst in history, so their punishment was also the worst in history. To call anything else "The Great Tribulation" is to downplay the immensity of that generation's crime.

Earnest Renan[21], an early writer said, "From this time forth, hunger, rage, despair, and madness dwelt in Jerusalem. It was a cage of furious maniacs, as city

---

[21] **Joseph Ernest Renan** (French: 28 February 1823 – 2 October 1892) was a French expert of the Middle East ancient languages and civilizations (philology), philosopher, historian, and writer, devoted to his native province of Brittany. He is best known for his influential historical works on early Christianity, and his political theories, especially concerning nationalism and national identity.

resounding with howling and inhabited by cannibals, a very hell. Titus, for his part, was atrociously vindictive; every day five hundred unfortunates were crucified in the sight of the city with hateful refinements of cruelty or sufficient ground whereon to erect them."[22]

Phillip Schaff[23], in his *History of the Christian Church*, gives us a vivid picture of the destruction of Jerusalem. "Titus (according to Josephus) intended, at first, to save that magnificent work of architecture, as a trophy of victory, and perhaps from some superstitious fear; and when the flames threatened to reach the Holy of Holies he forced his way through flame and smoke, over the dead and dying, to arrest the fire. But the destruction was determined by a higher decree. His own soldiers roused to madness by the stubborn resistance, and greedy of the golden treasures, could not be restrained from the work of destruction. At first, the halls around the temple were set on fire. Then a firebrand was hurled through the golden gate. When the flames arose the Jews raised a hideous yell, and tried to put out the fire; while others, clinging with a last convulsive grasp to their Messianic hopes, rested in the declaration of a false prophet, that God in the midst of the conflagration of the

---

[22] **Renan, Ernest** (2013). pp. 254-5. *Renan's Antichrist*. London: Forgotten Books. (Original work published 1900)

[23] **Philip Schaff** (January 1, 1819 – October 20, 1893), was a Swiss-born, German-educated Protestant theologian and a Church historian who spent most of his adult life living and teaching in the United States.

temple would give a signal for the deliverance of his people. The legions vied with each other in feeding the flames and made the unhappy people feel the full force of their unchained rage. Soon the whole prodigious structure was in a blaze and illuminated the skies. It was burned on the tenth of August, AD70, the same day of the year on which, according to tradition, the first temple was destroyed by Nebuchadnezzar." "No one", says Josephus, "can conceive of a louder, more terrible shriek than arose from all sides during the burning of the temple. The shout of victory and the jubilee of the legions sounded through the wailing of the people, now surrounded with fire and sword, upon the mountain, and throughout the city. The echo from all the mountains around, even to Perea, increased the deafening roar. Yet the misery itself was more terrible than this disorder. The hill on which the temple stood was seething hot and seemed enveloped to its base in one sheet of flame. The blood was larger in quantity than the fire, and those that were slain were more in number than those that slew them. The ground was nowhere visible. All was covered with corpses; over these heaps, the soldiers pursued the fugitives."[24] "The Romans planted their eagles on the shapeless ruins, over against the eastern gate, offered their sacrifices to them, and proclaimed Titus Imperator with the greatest acclamations of joy. Thus was fulfilled the prophecy concerning the abomination of desolation standing in the

---

[24] Copied from The Little Gleaner Vols. 5-6 Page 180

holy place." (Philip Schaff, vol. 1 pp. 397-398).

Can we even begin to realize the scope of the great tribulation upon the people of Israel? It was not just those in Jerusalem that suffered and died, but all over Palestine, the whole country felt the judgment of God. Josephus said, "There was not a Syrian city which did not slay their Jewish inhabitants, and were more bitter enemies to us than were the Romans themselves."

David Scott Clark said, "It is doubtful if anything before or since has equaled it for ruthless slaughter and merciless destruction. From the locality of these churches in Asia Minor to the borders of Egypt, the land was a slaughterhouse, city after city was wrecked, sacked, and burned; till it was recorded that cities were left without an inhabitant."[25]

The destruction of Jerusalem was far more than just the destruction of a city. Jerusalem and the temple were the center of worship of the one and only true and living God. With its destruction came a covenantal change. God's kingdom was taken from them, and no longer would the Jews or the Gentiles rule over God's kingdom because His kingdom was now a spiritual kingdom, entered not by a physical birth but by a spiritual

---

[25] Clark, David Scott. *The Message from Patmos*. 1879. Reprint. London: Forgotten Books, 2013. 54-5

birth. God had utterly destroyed the physical temple, the genealogical records which qualified descendants of Aaron to serve as priests, and the city of Jerusalem. The old system of worship was forever over. The destruction of Jerusalem was not simply a local judgment, it was a covenantal judgment. Notice Jesus' words in Matthew 23:35-36.

Matthew 23:35-36 (NIV)

35And so upon you will come all the righteous blood that has been shed on earth, from the blood of righteous Abel to the blood of Zechariah son of Berekiah, whom you murdered between the temple and the altar. 36Truly I tell you, all this will come on this generation.

This judgment upon Jerusalem was not simply local; it reached all the way back to Abel. The blood of Abel was vindicated by God's judgment upon Jerusalem. It was far more than the fall of a city, **it was the end of an age**. That is why Jesus said it would be a "great tribulation, such as has not been since the beginning of the world until this time, no, nor ever shall be". Jesus said nothing in time would ever equal what happened in AD70, nothing. He also said that this judgment would fall on "this generation". That means it was going to happen to some of those who were alive at that time, not thousands of years later. The Great Tribulation is behind us; it is an event in history. I hope you were able to get a glimpse of the enormity of this event.

Due the tremendous amount of interest and the number of books, movies, and proponents of the future expectation of a world war called the "Battle of Armageddon", it is important that you follow our understanding of this supposed future war in chapter 12 titled "The Battle of Armageddon".

NOTE: Josephus' quotes are from "Wars of The Jews".

Review

1. Is the tribulation in the future or has it already happened?
2. Why did God allow the devastation to Jerusalem in AD67 to AD70?
3. Are there any Scriptures which support the timing of the tribulation?
4. What was the "Abomination of Desolation"?

CHAPTER 4

THE THOUSAND YEARS

The third leg of the milk stool, mentioned in the introduction, is the belief and teaching by the dispensationalists concerning a 1000-year reign of Christ on this earth after a terrible seven-year period of tribulation upon Israel and the sinners that were left behind when the supposed rapture happened because of their unbelief. They further believe that after Christ returns at the end of the Great Tribulation, He will institute the thousand-year earthly rule from Jerusalem. Those who begin believing in Christ during the "seventieth week of Daniel" and survive the tribulation, as well as the unsaved, will go on to populate the earth during this time. Those raptured or raised prior to the tribulation will come back from heaven and reign with Christ over the earth for a thousand years. This view sees the re-establishment of temple worship and animal sacrifices as a remembrance of Christ's sacrifice.

The PTDs teach the 1000-years in Revelation chapter 20 is a time when Jesus will live on this earth and reign as king and ruler with His saints. After seriously reading Revelation 20:1-6, I simply cannot accept that teaching as fact. Let's look at the text and then see if we can more clearly understand what Jesus is saying here through John. Let's also look at what is not being said here.

The only time the "Millennium"[26] is mentioned specifically is in Revelation 20:1-6. It is called a "thousand years", not a millennium.

Revelation 20:1-6 (NIV)

[1]And I saw an angel coming down out of heaven, having the key to the Abyss and holding in his hand a great chain. [2]He seized the dragon, that ancient serpent, who is the devil, or Satan, and bound him for a thousand years. [3]He threw him into the Abyss, and locked and sealed it over him, to keep him from deceiving the nations anymore until the thousand years were ended. After that, he must be set free for a short time. [4]I saw thrones on which were seated those who had been given authority to judge. And I saw the souls of those who had been beheaded because of their testimony about Jesus and because of the word of God. They had not worshiped the beast or its image and had not received its mark on their foreheads or their hands. They came to life and reigned with Christ a thousand years. [5](The rest of the dead did not come to life until the thousand years were ended.) This is the first resurrection. [6]Blessed and holy are those who share in the first resurrection. The second death has no power over them, but they will be priests of God and of Christ and will reign with him for a thousand years.

---

[26] See Glossary for "Millennium"

How are we to understand this? Well, first the devil is a spirit. Are you going to chain a spirit with a real chain? So we have to admit that we are dealing with symbolism. Then the devil is cast into the abyss for a thousand years. The Lord shut him up and sealed him there so he could not deceive the nations for a thousand years. After that, he must be loosed for a season.

And John saw the thrones occupied by those who were beheaded for the witness of Jesus. They were given the right to rule. This suggests a victory for them. These martyrs, who had died, lived and reigned with Christ for a thousand years.

First notice that this passage says John saw the souls of them who were beheaded because of their testimony about Jesus. Did he see them physically or spiritually? Can you see a soul here on this earth? This is clearly a spiritual vision. Also, note that it doesn't say anything about other Christians, but only those who were martyred for the cause of Christ. Since most Christians were not killed for the cause of Christ, this certainly cannot mean most Christians are with the Lord during this 1000-year period of time. We will be addressing more about this particular issue later in the chapter.

Secondly, notice that this passage does not say where Christ and the saints reign. It has been a popular teaching by the dispensationalists that this happens here on this earth. It does not say that. If you believe that, it has many problems that need to be dealt with. As an example: if there is an earthly 1000-year reign, are there babies born in sin during that time? Is the Gospel preached and people saved or do they just continue to live as they always have? Does Jesus rule the earth with an iron hand? There are literally dozens of questions that cannot be answered by those who teach this mistaken view. I have asked just a few of the questions that need to be answered if you believe that Jesus is going to reign on this earth a thousand years.

What do you do with the Scripture that Jesus said about His earthly reign?

John 18:36 (NIV)

36 Jesus said, "My kingdom is not of this world. If it were, my servants would fight to prevent my arrest by the Jewish leaders. But now my kingdom is from another place."

Jesus had just taken the wind out of the disciples' sails with this statement. They were looking for Him to reign in an earthly kingdom. Isn't it ironic that we still have people today who are looking for Jesus to reign in an earthly kingdom?

Now let's look at more of this passage. But the rest of the dead lived not until the thousand years were finished. This is the first resurrection (vss.4-6). When the thousand years have expired, Satan is loosed out of his prison for a short time, to go and deceive the nations, and then he is forever cast into the lake of burning sulfur.

Revelation 20:10 (NIV)

¹⁰And the devil, who deceived them, was thrown into the lake of burning sulfur, where the beast and the false prophet had been thrown. They will be tormented day and night forever and ever.

Is the 1000-years literal or symbolical? Let's look at the term *thousand*. In every case where the term thousand years is used without an associated number, it is symbolical. Here are just a couple. II Peter 3:8 says that a day is with the Lord as a thousand years.

II Peter 3:8 (NIV)

⁸But do not forget this one thing, dear friends: With the Lord a day is like a thousand years, and a thousand years are like a day.

Let's look at Psalm 50:10. Can we be sure that it is exactly a thousand hills? NO! We must understand the symbolism in these passages. It's to emphasize a point and not an exact number.

Psalm 50:10 (NIV)

¹⁰for every animal of the forest is mine and the cattle on a thousand hills.

Now back to the passage we are looking at. If the rest of the passage in Revelation is symbolical, then the 1000-years must be also. You cannot separate the thousand years from who is reigning with Christ and make part of it literal and part of it symbolical.

Let's look at the "first resurrection".

Revelation 20:5 (NIV)

⁵(The rest of the dead did not come to life until the thousand years were ended.) This is the first resurrection.

John has been talking about the martyrs. Some see the "first resurrection" as one dying to sin and being raised to new life in Christ. But I believe that the first resurrection refers to the souls of the martyrs. They died, yet they are living on in heaven. Now when you have a first, you also have a second. So actually, I see the second resurrection as the final resurrection of which Christ spoke, and of which Paul spoke in I Corinthians 15 and I Thessalonians 4, and other Scriptures, that will occur at the second coming of Christ. We've already addressed when the second resurrection happens in the chapter regarding when the "rapture" takes place.

Revelation 20:13 (NIV)

¹³The sea gave up the dead that were in it, and death and Hades gave up the dead that were in them, and each person was judged according to what they had done. [14]Then death and Hades were thrown into the lake of fire. The lake of fire is the second death. [15]Anyone whose name was not found written in the book of life was thrown into the lake of fire.

As for the final judgment itself, note that it includes all people, which means Christians and non-Christians. This judgment, while including the Christians, will not determine whether one is saved and will go to heaven, but will determine their rewards. It only reveals the fact that one's final destination is fixed the moment he dies or when the Lord returns. Those whose names are in "the book of life" (vs.15) go to heaven. All others go to hell and eternal punishment.

The pre-millennialists believe that the book of Revelation, where the only time the millennium or thousand years is mentioned, is written in chronological order and the millennium must be interpreted literally and chronologically. They would say that the events in Revelation 20 follow the vision of the second coming of Christ, which is pictured in Rev. 19:11-16.

Revelation 19:11-16 (NIV)

[11]I saw heaven standing open and there before me was a white horse, whose rider is called Faithful and True. With justice, he judges and wages war. [12]His eyes are like blazing fire, and on his head are many crowns. He has a name written on him that no one knows but he himself. [13]He is dressed in a robe dipped in blood, and his

name is the Word of God. ¹⁴The armies of heaven were following him, riding on white horses and dressed in fine linen, white and clean. ¹⁵Coming out of his mouth is a sharp sword with which to strike down the nations. "He will rule them with an iron scepter." He treads the winepress of the fury of the wrath of God Almighty. ¹⁶On his robe and on his thigh he has this name written: KING OF KINGS AND LORD OF LORDS."

I cannot agree that chapter 20 follows chronologically what is described in chapter 19, any more than what is described in Revelation 12 (the birth of the man-child, Christ) follows chronologically what is described in the last verse of chapter 11 (the judging of the dead and the giving of rewards to the saints). Please compare those verses.

Revelation 11:17-18 (NIV)

¹⁷saying: "We give thanks to you, Lord God Almighty, the One who is and who was because you have taken your great power and have begun to reign.¹⁸The nations were angry, and your wrath has come. The time has come for judging the dead, and for rewarding your servants the prophets and your people who revere your name, both great and small and for destroying those who destroy the earth."

I'm only showing this as an example that you cannot take all of Revelation and treat it chronologically. If you interpret the entire Revelation as running chronologically, you would have to say that Christ was born after the second coming and the judgment of saints and sinners, because Revelation 12 follows Revelation 11. What you have in Revelation 12 is the author going back and starting with the beginning of the church age and continuing through the entire church age to the second coming for the fourth time (Revelation chapters 12-14). We will not deal with all of these passages here, but I will specifically deal with the Beast mentioned in chapter 13 in another chapter titled "Introduction to Understanding Revelation".

Actually, Revelation 20:1-6 takes us back to the beginning of the entire church age and continues to the second coming for the seventh and final time (Revelation 20-22). You cannot take Revelation chronologically, but must understand that it has many parallel sequences in it. The chapter in this book titled "You Can't Read Revelation Chronologically" will help explain how the book should be viewed. If you wish to pursue this idea further, I highly recommend Dr. Howard Hendrickson's book *"More than Conquerors"* for a great example of how the book of Revelation should be viewed. Also, section three on "Understanding Revelation" in this book will greatly help in clarifying much of the confusion associated with many misunderstandings of those who try to teach a pre-millennial approach to the events recorded in John's apocalyptic[27] writings.

When referring to the binding of Satan in Revelation 20:1-6, most pre-millennial teachers do not tell us exactly what the "binding" is and they do not compare the "binding" in Revelation 20 with Jesus' teachings in Matthew 12:29. Let's look at that passage.

Matthew 12:29 (NIV)

[29]*"Or again, how can anyone enter a strong man's house and carry off his possessions unless he first ties up the strong man? Then he can plunder his house."*

The proper interpretation of Revelation 20:1-6 is that it appears Satan has been bound in his attempt to deceive the nations. Jesus actually set the binding of Satan in motion when He overcame the devil's temptation in the wilderness (See Matthew chapter 4). Satan has been bound for a long period of time (the church age) which is the true meaning of the millennium as we will see shortly. Yet, Revelation reveals that Satan at the end of the church age, shortly before the second coming, will be released from the pit during a brief period of time, often referred to wrongly as the "Great Tribulation" to deceive the world. I believe it is certainly possible we may now be living in the time when Satan has

---

[27] See Glossary for the definition of apocalyptic

been loosed for a season which is referenced at the start of this chapter in Revelation 20:3.

In Revelation 20 this deception is not called the "Great Tribulation" and nothing is said about it being 7 years in duration. Interestingly enough, the word used by Matthew in chapter 12 verse 29 to describe the binding of the strong man is the same word that is used in Revelation 20 to describe the binding of Satan. Now let's have a closer look at Revelation 20:1-6. In these verses, we have a description of the binding of Satan. The dragon, here clearly identified as "the devil, or Satan", is said to be bound for a thousand years and cast into a place called "the Abyss". The purpose of the binding is "to keep him from deceiving the nations" anymore until the thousand years, or church age were ended. For those who have rejected the Gospel, Paul writes the following:

II Thessalonians 2:11 (NIV)

11For this reason, God sends them a powerful delusion so that they will believe the lie.

What lie? The lie of the devil is when he will be set free at the end of the thousand years for a short time to deceive the nations. They will believe the lie of the devil because they have not accepted the truth of the Gospel. Paul encourages the believers to stand fast and hold to the traditions they have been taught. They will not be fooled by the lie written in II Thessalonians 2:11.

It is obvious from reading all of Second Thessalonians chapter 2[28], something very devastating is going to happen to those who have chosen not to follow the truth but have pleasure in unrighteousness. This passage could easily be referring to Revelation 20:3 where it states "After that, he must be set free for a short time." Revelation addresses this deception or lie with the following:

Revelation 20:7-8 (NIV)

[7]When the thousand years are over, Satan will be released from his prison[8] and will go out to deceive the nations in the four corners of the earth—Gog and Magog—and to gather them for battle. In number, they are like the sand on the seashore.

The book of Revelation is full of symbolic numbers. Obviously, the number "thousand" which is used here must not be interpreted in a literal sense. Since the number ten signifies completeness, and since a thousand is ten to the third power, we may think of the expression "a thousand years" as standing for a complete but very long period of indeterminate length. In agreement with what was said above about the structure of Revelation and in the light of verses 7-15 of chapter 20, which describe Satan's little season including the final battle and the final judgment, we may conclude that this thousand-

---

[28] Please read II Thessalonians chapter 2 for clarity regarding Revelation chapter 20:8

year period extends from Christ's first coming to just before His second coming.

Since the "lake of fire" mentioned in verses 10, 14 and 15 is obviously a description of the place of final punishment, the "Abyss" mentioned in verses 1 and 3 must not be the place of final punishment. The word *Abyss* should rather be thought of as a figurative description of the way in which Satan's activities will be curbed or limited during the thousand-year period.

Just before His ascension, however, Christ gave His disciples the Great Commission in Matthew:

Matthew 28:19-20 (NIV)

[19]Therefore go and make disciples of all nations, baptizing them in the name of the Father and of the Son and of the Holy Spirit, [20] and teaching them to obey everything I have commanded you. And surely I am with you always, to the very end of the age."

At this point, we can well imagine the disciples raising a disturbing question. How can we possibly do this if Satan continues to deceive the nations the way he has in the past? In Revelation 20:1-3 John gives a reassuring answer to the question.

Revelation 20:1-3 (NIV)

¹And I saw an angel coming down out of heaven, having the key to the Abyss and holding in his hand a great chain. ²He seized the dragon, that ancient serpent, who is the devil, or Satan, and bound him for a thousand years. ³He threw him into the Abyss, and locked and sealed it over him, to keep him from deceiving the nations anymore until the thousand years were ended. After that, he must be set free for a short time.

Satan will not be able to deceive the nations while the church is fulfilling the "Great Commission" written in Matthew 28:19-20, because he is bound and greater is He [Christ] that is within you than he [Satan] that is in the world.

I John 4:4 (NIV)

⁴You, dear children, are from God and have overcome them, because the one who is in you is greater than the one who is in the world.

This does not imply that Satan cannot do any harm because he is bound. It means only what John says here: While Satan is bound he cannot deceive the nations in such a way as to keep them from learning about the truth of God. Later we are told that when the thousand years are over, Satan will be released from his prison and will go out to deceive the nations of the world and gather them together to fight against and, if possible, to destroy the people of God (verses 7-9). This, however, cannot be while he is bound. We conclude, then, that the binding of Satan during the Gospel age means that, first, he cannot prevent the spread of the Gospel, and second, he cannot gather all the enemies of Christ together to attack the church.

Is there any indication in the New Testament that Satan was bound at the time of the first coming of Christ? Indeed, there is. When the Pharisees accused Jesus of casting out demons by the power of Satan, Jesus replied:

Matthew 12:28 (NIV)

28But if it is by the Spirit of God that I drive out demons, then the kingdom of God has come upon you.

It is precisely because the Kingdom of God has come that the Gospel can be preached to all nations. Satan is bound during this period of the church age and cannot prevent the spreading of the Gospel.

Luke 10:17-18 (NIV)

17The seventy-two returned with joy and said, "Lord, even the demons submit to us in your name." 18He replied, "I saw Satan fall like lightning from heaven".

These words, needless to say, must not be interpreted literally. They must rather be understood to mean that Jesus saw in the works His disciples were doing an indication that Satan's kingdom had just been dealt a crushing blow. The binding of Satan and the restriction of his power had just taken place. In this instance, Satan's fall or binding is associated directly with the missionary activity of Jesus' disciples.

Another passage which ties into the restriction of Satan's activities with Christ's missionary outreach is John 12:31-32.

John 12:31-32 (NIV)

31Now is the time for judgment on this world; now the prince of this world will be driven out. 32And I, when I am lifted up from the earth, will draw all people to myself."

It is interesting to note that the verb here translated "driven out" *(ekballo)* is derived from the same root as the word used in Revelation 20:3, "He [the angel] threw *[ballo]* him [Satan] into the abyss." Even more important, however, is the observation that Satan's being "driven out" (NIV) is here associated with the fact that not only the Jews but the men of all nationalities shall be drawn to Christ as He hangs upon the cross.

We see then that the binding of Satan, though certainly not annihilated, is so curtailed that he cannot prevent the spread of the Gospel to the nations of the world. When the apostles were given the "keys", which is the Gospel of Christ, they had power over the works of Satan. We will win the battle even though Satan is working to defeat us. Look at the following Scriptures.

Matthew 16:18-19 (NIV)

18And I tell you that you are Peter and on this rock I will build my church, and the gates of Hades will not overcome it. 19 I will give you the keys of the kingdom of heaven; whatever you bind on earth will be bound in heaven, and whatever you loose on earth will be loosed in heaven."

Matthew 24:14 (NIV)

14And this Gospel of the kingdom will be preached in the whole world as a testimony to all nations, and then the end will come.

When we add to this consideration the fact that John sees the souls of those who had been beheaded, we have confirmed that the location of John's vision has shifted to heaven. The souls, since this is a spiritual viewing, are obviously seen somewhere other than on earth. We may say then the thousand-year period described in Revelation chapter 20:1-6 (found near the beginning of this chapter) is showing what is happening both here on earth and in heaven. Verses 1-3 are describing what is happening on earth during this time and verses 4-6 are depicting what is happening in heaven at the same time.

The martyrs in these verses are representative of all who die as martyrs throughout the various persecutions of the church age. When John wrote Revelation, many Christians were being martyred for their faith. Needless to say, the apocalyptic vision recorded in Revelation chapter 20:4 would bring great comfort to the relatives and friends of these martyrs.

The dispensationalists wrongly teach that this 1000-years is after the invisible coming of Christ and the rapture of the church. They teach Jesus will rule the earth from Jerusalem when He returns during this one thousand-year period. They further say the Jewish nation will be restored, another temple is rebuilt, sacrifices renewed and that during this period the Jewish nation will rule over the land of Israel from Jerusalem, under the authority of Jesus. However, there is not one mention of a rebuilt temple, or Israel as a nation, or the land in any place in the Bible. Again, this is something the PTD teachers are just simply assuming.

I believe the millennium (1000-years) is the New Testament church age, which will last an indefinite period of time and will be full and complete at the time of Christ's final and only literal return. This makes it a millennium that is being realized now or a "realized millennium"[29].

Although this is my own belief, I wish to share it here. Please realize I am not setting any specific date because none of us know the actual timing of the events, and at best, may be able to see what is happening as an indicator of the "Last Days". Understanding that the 1000-years (indefinite time period) is the church age or the time from the Lord's earthly appearance until near the end, I believe we could now be in the time when Satan has been loosed and is attacking believers like never before.

The Realized Millennium[30]

Now let's look at what most of those, including me, who believe in a realized millennium teach to clear up possible confusion.

The following is what I don't believe.
1. I do not deny the existence of a millennium.
2. I do not believe that everything is symbolized in the Bible.
3. I do not have a non-literal understanding of the Bible.
4. I do not hold to a literal future "golden age" on earth.
5. I do not believe in "replacement theology"[31].
6. I am not in any way anti-Semitic or anti-Jewish.

---

[29] See Glossary on a-millennialism
[30] Many of the following points in this section can be found at Preteristarchive.com posted by Jason Robertson.
[31] See glossary for replacement theology

Now let's look at what I do believe about the Bible.

1. I believe that it follows a grammatical-historical-literal interpretation of the Scriptures which includes many symbolic interpretations. As an example, those of us who believe in a realized millennium understand that Galatians 4:21-31 is literally requiring its readers to recognize the symbolic or "spiritual" lessons God taught us in Genesis with reference to Sarah and Hagar. Such literal interpretive principles leads us to conclude that Israel as an ethnic group in the OT was real but typological spiritually. Abraham's true offspring or true "Israel" has nothing to do with a person's ethnicity, but refers to one's faith (Galatians 3:29).

2. I believe that the whole Bible is a unit and contains no contradictions.

3. I believe there is no "gap" in Daniel's prophecy of Seventy Weeks, but that it was fulfilled with the desolation of the Temple and destruction of Jerusalem by Titus and the Roman army in AD70 (as the Tribulation judgment against non-believing Israel).

4. I believe explicitly in the millennium of Revelation 20 as a complete period of time, but the length is known only by God, and that the millennial kingdom of Christ began with His incarnation and will consummate at His second coming. It is properly called a "Realized Millennium".

5. I believe that the millennium is the present church age and spiritual reign of Christ on earth, as well as with His saints in heaven.

6. I believe that every person who is born again, both Jew and Gentile, immediately becomes a child of the King and has been given the right to reign with the King.
7. I believe that although he cannot prevail against the church, Satan still goes about as a roaring lion, in a limited capacity, tempting, defying, deceiving, until Christ shall put him down finally at His second coming.
8. I believe that good and evil will exist side by side until the harvest, which Jesus said will be the end of the world (Matt. 13:39).
9. I believe that Satan will be allowed to mount one final climactic antichrist rebellion and apostasy just before the second coming (Revelation 16:14; 20:7, 8). (I believe that we may in fact be seeing the beginning of that last rebellion.)
10. I believe that the first resurrection was when the martyrs were resurrected which is recorded in Rev. 20:5.
11. I believe in only one last trump and the second resurrection which will happen at the same time as the Lord's second coming.
12. I believe the second coming of Christ will be a literal, visible to all, bodily coming. (no secret coming here)
13. I believe that, at the second coming, all the saints both living and dead, will meet the Lord, and be given new spiritual bodies.

14. I believe that the millennium will end with the second coming of Christ followed by the judgments of the living and the dead, both saved and lost (Matt. 13:24-30; 47-53), and the creation of a new heaven and earth will follow after the judgment.
15. I believe in an imminent and any moment return of Christ.
16. I view the second coming as the consummation of the redemption story.

As I bring this chapter to a close, I want to address a very serious issue. When a church stops preaching the Gospel and winning the lost, that church is open to the destruction of Satan and any church that fails to fulfill the Great Commission will become weak, divided and die. The power of the Gospel preached and lived out in the lives of its members is a restraining force against the wiles and attacks of Satan. One thing all dysfunctional churches have in common is they have stopped 'making disciples' for Christ, which includes winning the lost. Making disciples is to follow the Lord's instruction. We should be leading them to Christ and teaching them in spiritual matters, using the Bible and other teaching tools.

Conclusion

Most of Revelation takes its symbols and references from the Old Testament. This would explicitly show that those who knew the Old Testament would understand Revelation.

1. Why would the writer use symbols?
2. Is there a literal thousand years?
3. Do the Scriptures tell us where the reign of Christ is or will be?
4. Are the souls mentioned in Revelation chapter 20 physical or spiritual?
5. Are all Christians who have died at this time included?
6. Can part of a verse be taken literal while the rest is spiritual?
7. What does the Scripture imply when it says that Satan will be loosed?
8. Are there any signs that must be fulfilled before Christ returns?

CHAPTER 5

MATTHEW 24 AND THE END OF THE AGE

Why is it important that we look specifically at this passage of Scripture?

Dispensationalists believe that this prophecy taught by Jesus is talking about a seven-year period of tribulation on this earth that is still in the future. I totally disagree with that belief and will explain why in this chapter. Even though much of the chapter is dealing with the Gospel being preached in the world, toward the end of this chapter I will address several things that Jesus teaches in Matthew chapter 24 that have nothing to do with a "future" seven-year period of tribulation.

Let's look at the prophecies that Jesus taught the disciples in Matthew 24. We will deal with most of them, but in particular, His statement regarding the Gospel of the kingdom being preached in all the world before the end comes.

Matthew 24:14 (NIV)

[14]And this Gospel of the kingdom will be preached in the whole world as a testimony to all nations, and then the end will come.

Notice that the Greek word for world here is "oi)koume/nh" (which means in all the inhabited earth).

Before the destruction of Jerusalem, the Gospel had been carried into all parts of the then known world.

"Then the end will come." The end of what? What were they asking about? The destruction of the temple and the end of the Jewish age. Jesus is not saying the world will end when everyone has heard the Gospel. Jesus very clearly tells His disciples that before the temple would be destroyed and before His parousia and the end of the covenant age, the Gospel must be preached in all the world. And it was. The temple was destroyed in AD70. He arrived in His full glory in a judgmental coming, not a physical coming! The Old Covenant age ended. Then shall the end come, and indeed it did. The end of the Jewish economy and the destruction of the temple and city happened. Look at our chapter titled "The Great Tribulation" for all of the details of that horrible and devastating time for the Jews.

This does not mean that the Gospel was or is not to be preached after the end of the age had come. It was to be preached forever and always until the Lord visibly and physically returns on that "last day" when the "last trumpet" sounds. I hope that you are faithfully proclaiming this message to everyone who is thirsty – come, drink of the waters of life and you will never thirst again!

We are not sure about the efforts of most of the apostles, but we know from Paul's writings we can say that very few quarters of the Roman world were left unvisited. Paul supports, in Romans 10:14-18, what Jesus said in Matthew 24:14.

Romans 10:14-18 (NIV)

[14]How, then, can they call on the one they have not believed in? And how can they believe in the one of whom they have not heard? And how can they hear without someone preaching to them? [15]And how can anyone preach unless they are sent? As it is written: "How beautiful are the feet of those who bring good news!" [16]But not all the Israelites accepted the good news. For Isaiah says, "Lord, who has believed our message?" [17]Consequently, faith comes from hearing the message, and the message is heard through the word about Christ. [18]But I ask: Did they not hear? Of course, they did: "Their voice has gone out into all the earth, their words to the ends of the world."

"Their voice has gone out into all the earth, their words to the ends of the world." Paul uses the exact same Greek word for "world" that Jesus did in Matthew 24:14. He says that the Gospel was preached to every kingdom under heaven in Col. 1:5-6 and vs 23.

Colossians 1:5-6 (NIV)

[5]the faith and love that spring from the hope stored up for you in heaven and about which you have already heard in the true message of the Gospel [6]that has come

80

to you. In the same way, the Gospel is bearing fruit and growing throughout the whole world—just as it has been doing among you since the day you heard it and truly understood God's grace.

Colossians 1:23 (NIV)

23if you continue in your faith, established and firm, and do not move from the hope held out in the Gospel. This is the Gospel that you heard and that has been proclaimed to every creature under heaven, and of which I, Paul, have become a servant.

In these passages as well as others, Paul uses the Greek word "kosmos" which by implication means the earth and its inhabitants. For further support of this, he himself carried it to Arabia, Syria, Asia Minor, Greece, Illyricum, Rome, Spain. Look at Romans 15:19, 24, 28; Galatians 1:17; Philippians 1:13.

The concept is that both Jews and Gentiles have the opportunity of receiving or rejecting Christ. The witness should be for or against them according to the use made of this opportunity. At least by implication here, the Gospel has been presented to the then known world which fulfills the prophecy by Jesus in Matthew 24:14. Jesus says, "then the end shall come". Here is the question. What end is Jesus referring to? We will look into this further later in this chapter. Let's now look at several commentaries regarding Matthew 24:14. I will modify or shorten some of them for the sake of time. It will in no way change the meaning of what the writers are saying to us.

Matthew 24:3-5 (NIV)

³As Jesus was sitting on the Mount of Olives, the disciples came to him privately. "Tell us," they said, "when will this happen, and what will be the sign of your coming and of the end of the age?" ⁴Jesus answered: "Watch out that no one deceives you. ⁵ For many will come in my name, claiming, 'I am the Messiah,' and will deceive many.

Please keep this in mind; Jesus is speaking to His disciples. Whatever Jesus' answer means, it must have meaning to them. Any application that we make to ourselves from Scripture can only be made after we understand what it meant to the original audience. Keep in mind the principle of who He was talking to. Why is this important?   Because many today miss it. Dispensationalists view Matthew 24:4-14 as events of the church age leading up to the tribulation (which they view as yet to come). They say these signs indicate that the end of the age is approaching in our time. The end of the age, not the world, happened in AD70. Jesus was teaching His disciples what would happen before

Jerusalem fell and the temple was destroyed.

James Stuart Russell in his book, "*The Parousia*", says this on Matthew 24:4-14, "It is impossible to read this section and fail to perceive its distinct reference to the period between our Lord's crucifixion and the destruction of Jerusalem. Every word is spoken to the disciples, and to them alone. To imagine that the "ye" and "you" in this address apply, not to the disciples to whom Christ was speaking, but to some unknown and yet non-existent persons in a far distant age is so preposterous a supposition as not to deserve serious notice."

The Lord begins with a warning against expecting His immediate parousia. He doesn't want them to be deceived by false Christs that would soon be appearing. He wants them to understand that He will be gone for what might seem to them a long time. Jesus said between His departure at the ascension and His second coming, these are the things that would be happening to them.

Luke 21:8 (NIV)

8He replied: "Watch out that you are not deceived. For many will come in my name, claiming, 'I am he,' and, 'The time is near.' Do not follow them.

Luke adds the phrase "the time is near". Jesus was not talking about something that would take place hundreds or thousands of years later. Jesus was warning His disciples about something that was drawing very near in their time.

A. False Messiahs

Did such false Messiahs arise and deceive many in those years before the destruction of Jerusalem? Yes! We have a biblical and historical record of many such false Messiahs.

Acts 5:36-37 supports what Josephus, the Jewish historian, said twelve years after our Lord's death: Theudas persuaded a great multitude to follow him to the river Jordan which he claimed would divide for their passage. "The land", says Josephus, "was overrun with magicians, seducers, and impostors, who drew the people after them in multitudes into solitude and deserts, to see the signs and miracles which they promised to show by the power of God." At the time of Felix (who is mentioned in Acts 23-25), the country of the Jews was filled with impostors who Felix had put to death every day. An Egyptian who "pretended to be a prophet" gathered 30,000 men, claiming he would show "how, at his command, the walls of Jerusalem would fall down". Origen mentions a certain wonder-worker, Dositheus, who claimed he was the Christ foretold by Moses.

We see another of these false Christs in Acts 8:9-11. In Matthew 24:4 (KJV) Jesus said "take heed that no man deceive you", yet these Samaritans "all gave heed" to Simon because of his signs and wonders, from the least to the greatest, thus fulfilling Christ's words, "and shall deceive many". According to Irenaeus, Simon claimed to be the Son of God and creator of angels. Jerome says that he claimed to be the Word of God, the Almighty. Justin relates that he went to Rome and was acclaimed as a god by his magical powers.

John, who heard Jesus give this prophecy, recorded the fulfillment in 1 John 2:18, 22; 4:1 and 2 John 7. Notice how John, writing around AD65, doesn't say it is the "last days" but the "last hour".

I John 2:18 (NIV)

[18]Dear children, this is the last hour; and as you have heard that the antichrist is coming, even now many antichrists have come. This is how we know it is the last hour.

These are examples of the false Messiahs of whom history says there were "a great number", and of whom Jesus had prophesied that there would be "many".

B. Wars and Rumors of Wars

Matthew 24:6 (NIV)

[6]You will hear of wars and rumors of wars but see to it that you are not alarmed. Such things must happen, but the end is still to come.

Wars are not a sign of the end, as the last part of

verse 6 clearly tells us. He will tell them later in this chapter that when they see a war, not hear of one, they are to flee. Did the disciples hear of wars, rumors of wars? Yes, they did! Josephus said, in Antiquities 18:5:3, that Bardanes, and after him Volageses, declared war against Aretas, King of Arabia. But the death of Tiberius prevented war (rumors of war). There were wars in the tributaries of Rome and all over Palestine, Galilee, and Samaria in AD66, preceding the destruction of Jerusalem.

In the records of Tacitus[32], a Roman who wrote a history which covers the period prior to AD70, we find such expressions as these: "Disturbances in Germany", "commotions in Africa", "commotions in Thrace", "insurrections in Gaul", "intrigues among the Parthians", "the war in Britain", "war in Armenia".

Among the Jews, the times became turbulent. In Seleucia, 50,000 Jews were killed. There was an uprising against them in Alexandria. In a battle between the Jews and Syrians in Caesarea, 20,000 were killed. During these times, Caligula ordered his statue placed in the temple at

---

[32] **Publius** (or **Gaius**) **Cornelius Tacitus**; Classical Latin: ['takɪtʊs]; c. AD 56 – after 117) was a senator and a historian of the Roman Empire. The surviving portions of his two major works—the Annals and the Histories examine the reigns of the Roman Emperors Tiberius, Claudius, Nero, and those who reigned in the Year of the Four Emperors(AD 69). These two works span the history of the Roman Empire from the death of Augustus in AD 14 to the years of the First Jewish/Roman War in AD70. There are substantial gaps in the surviving texts, including a gap in theAnnals that is four books long.

86

Jerusalem. The Jews refused to do this and lived in constant fear that the Emperor's armies would be sent into Palestine. This fear became so real that some of them did not even bother to till their fields.

But though there would be wars and rumors of wars, Jesus told His disciples: "See that ye be not troubled: for all these things must come to pass, but the end is not yet." What end is He talking about? Let's keep in mind their question: they wanted to know when the end of the Jewish age would come. Barnes says the end here referred to is, "the end of the Jewish economy; the destruction of Jerusalem".[33]

Wars and rumors of wars were not signs of the end; to the contrary, the Lord wanted them to know that these things were not signs of the end. None of these things would be the sign which would cause the disciples to flee into the mountains.

C. Nation fighting Nation

Matthew 24:7 (NIV)

[7]Nation will rise against nation and kingdom against kingdom. There will be famines and earthquakes in various places.

The word "nation" here is the Greek word ethnos, which means, a race. There are those who say this is talking about race wars and this verse proves that we are

---

[33] Barnes Notes on the New Testament Page 114

in the end times and the second coming will be soon. There are several problems with that view, one of which is these things are not signs of the end of the world, but of the age. Also, Jesus was speaking to the disciples; this had to have relevance to them. Did they see nation rising against nation? Yes! Josephus says, "At Caesarea in AD59 the Jews and Syrians contended about the right to the city, and twenty thousand Jews were slain. At Scythopolis, over 13,000 Jews were killed. Thousands were killed in other places, and at Alexandria 50,000 were killed. At Damascus, 10,000 were killed in an hour's time."[34] Jesus is speaking about the conflicts between Gentiles and Jews, which began to take place shortly after this time. For some time previously, Gentiles and Jews had been living for the most part in peace together, but this period was distinguished by wars.

D. Famines

Acts 11:28 (NIV)

[28]One of them, named Agabus, stood up and through the Spirit predicted that a severe famine would spread over the entire Roman world. (This happened during the reign of Claudius.)

Historians record 30,000 deaths in Rome alone. This famine is mentioned by Tacitus, Suetonius, and Eusebius, and is said to have been severe in Jerusalem.

---

[34] Barnes notes on the New Testament Chapter XXIV Page 113

Josephus says that many people perished for want of food. Judea was especially hard hit by famine and the disciples sent aid to them (Acts 11:27-29). Tacitus speaks of a "failure in the crops, and a famine consequent thereupon". Eusebius also mentions famines during this time in Rome, Judea, and Greece. The Bible records famines (Acts 11:27-29) which occurred during the reign of Claudius in AD41-AD54. There were famines in those years before the fall of Jerusalem.

E. Pestilence

Suetonius wrote of "pestilence" at Rome in the days of Nero which was so severe that "within the space of one autumn there died no less than 30,000 persons". Josephus records that pestilences raged in Babylonia in AD40. Tacitus tells of pestilences in Italy in AD65. There were pestilences in the lifetime of the disciples in those years leading up to the destruction of Jerusalem.

F. Earthquakes

Did the disciples experience earthquakes in their lifetime? Yes! Tacitus mentions earthquakes at Rome. He wrote, "Frequent earthquakes occurred, by which many houses were thrown down", and "twelve populous cities of Asia fell in ruins from an earthquake."[35]

Seneca, writing in the year AD58, said, "How often have cities of Asia and Achaea fallen with one fatal shock!

---

[35] The Bible Verified by Rev. Andrew Archibald, Presbyterian board of Publication and Sabbath-School Work Page 186

How many cities have been swallowed up in Syria! How many in Macedonia! How often has Cyprus been wasted by this calamity! How often has Paphos become a ruin! News has often been brought us of the demolition of whole cities at once."[36] In AD60, Hierapous, Colosse, and Laodicea were overthrown from earthquakes. There were earthquakes in Crete, Apamea, Smyrna, Miletus, Chios, Samos, and Judea as well as other places.

History records earthquakes in Crete AD46, Rome AD51, Apamaia AD53, Laodicea AD60, and Campania AD62. The Bible records earthquakes in many places after Jesus' prediction and before AD70 (Mat.27:51; 28:2, Acts 16:26).

In spite of what Jesus said, "the end is not yet", many today take this passage out of context and speak ignorantly about "the signs of the times", trying to show that present day battles, serious earthquakes, or devastating famines are a sign of Christ's imminent return. All of these things happened in the time prior to AD70 and the fall of Jerusalem. As we look back over history, has there ever been a time when there were not wars, famines, pestilence and earthquakes? These things are not the final signs. Jesus said to His disciples that these things are just the "beginning of sorrows" (Matthew 24:8), not the end.

The phrase "beginning of sorrows" could be

---

[36] ibid

translated "birth pains". This image is sometimes used in the Old Testament simply to express great pain, but it is often used of a woman in the pain of childbirth. In Isaiah 13:8 and 26:17, Jeremiah 4:31and 6:24, Micah 4:9-10, it is used almost as a special term for "the birth pains of Messiah". In our passage, it speaks of the period of distress preceding the return (not a literal coming) of Christ in judgment on the Jews in AD70. Its use here is expressly chosen to denote the birth pains of a new world.

Let's look at how Jesus uses this phrase in John 16:16. The disciples question Jesus about His statement (John 16:17-19). Jesus explains Himself in John 16:20-23.

John 16:16-23 (NIV)

[16]Jesus went on to say, "In a little while you will see me no more, and then after a little while, you will see me." [17]At this, some of his disciples said to one another, "What does he mean by saying, 'In a little while you will see me no more, and then after a little while you will see me,' and Because I am going to the Father'?" [18]They kept asking, "What does he mean by 'a little while'? We don't understand what he is saying." [19]Jesus saw that they wanted to ask him about this, so he said to them, "Are you asking one another what I meant when I said, 'In a little while you will see me no more, and then after a little while you will see me'? [20]Very truly I tell you, you

will weep and mourn while the world rejoices. You will grieve, but your grief will turn to joy. [21]A woman giving birth to a child has pain because her time has come, but when her baby is born she forgets the anguish because of her joy that a child is born into the world. [22]So with you: Now is your time of grief, but I will see you again and you will rejoice, and no one will take away your joy. [23]In that day, you will no longer ask me anything. Very truly I tell you, my Father will give you whatever you ask in my name.

The disciples would be sorrowful during the Lord's absence but their sorrow would turn to joy at His return. This idea of a woman in labor is used for the suffering that precedes the coming of the Lord in His kingdom (Micah 4:9-10).

Jesus said, "All these are the beginning of sorrows." They were not signs to the disciples and they are not signs today. They did not signal the end but stretches over the entire period between the Lord's ascension and second coming which I call the church age.

G. Disciples Persecuted

Matthew 24:9 (NIV)

[9]*"Then you will be handed over to be persecuted and put to death, and you will be hated by all nations because of me.*

92

Who will be delivered up and killed? The disciples. Now it is certainly true that all Christians who live a godly life will suffer persecution, but He is speaking to the disciples here. Did the disciples experience tribulation and death? Yes! All you need to do is read the book of Acts.

Dispensationalists have this to say about verse 9: "Jesus began His words with a time word, 'Then'. At the middle point of the seven-year period preceding Christ's second coming, great distress will begin to be experienced by Israel." They are saying that Jesus is talking about a time still future to us. Would this mean anything to the disciples? Certainly not. Not only do they fail to take into account audience relevance here, but they fail to compare the other Gospel accounts with this one. Let's look at what Luke has to say.

Luke 21:12 (NIV)

12 "But before all this, they will seize you and persecute you. They will hand you over to synagogues and put you in prison, and you will be brought before kings and governors, and all on account of my name.

Luke adds, "Before all these things", showing that persecutions are to start at the beginning of this period. The persecution of the disciples began immediately after the day of Pentecost. Here's what Mark has to say:

Mark 13:9 (NIV)

⁹"You must be on your guard. You will be handed over to the local councils and flogged in the synagogues. On account of me, you will stand before governors and kings as witnesses to them.

Mark adds that they will be beaten in the synagogues, brought before rulers and kings as witnesses. All this was remarkably fulfilled in the lives of the disciples. The apostles were constantly threatened by the Pharisees and told not to teach in the Lord's name. Peter and John were imprisoned. So were many of the other apostles. Paul and Silas were beaten and imprisoned. The Jews laid hands on Paul to kill him and brought him before the Pharisees and the Sadducees, and then brought him before governors, then Felix and King Agrippa, and Gallio, which fulfills Matthew 10:18 as well. As soon as Paul began preaching, he began to experience persecution. Paul was stoned and beaten and thrown into prison. He was beaten by the Jews several times.

Jesus said the disciples would be afflicted, beaten, imprisoned; they would be hated for His name's sake and some would be killed. They would be brought before councils, rulers, and kings, for a testimony; they would be given a mouth of wisdom which their adversaries could not dispute. The disciples experienced all of this before the fall of Jerusalem in AD70, just as the Lord said they would. The prophecy was fulfilled in every detail.

H. False Prophets

Matthew 24:11 (NIV)

11and many false prophets will appear and deceive many people.

The early historic records show there were many false prophets during the time of the disciples. The testimony of Josephus shows the utter lawlessness of the Jewish society in the disciples' lifetime.

This chapter should clear up a lot of misunderstanding regarding Jesus' teaching to the disciples. As you can see, this is not something that is just happening in the 21st century, but all of these things occurred before Jerusalem fell in AD70. That is not to say there haven't been other occurrences of similar events and even similarities happening today. This is simply addressing the fact that these prophecies, told by Jesus, did occur from the time He told the disciples about them before the destruction of Jerusalem. Jesus is teaching the disciples they would see and experience these things before they died.

Conclusion

In this chapter, Jesus tells His disciples that the Gospel will be preached to the "then known world". "oi)koume/nh" (which means in all the inhabited earth).

Paul confirms that point in Romans chapter 10.

The end would come shortly after this happened.

When was the Lord's Parousia?

Did God terminate His covenant with Jews?

Jesus prophesied about the following:

- False Messiahs would come in His name
- Wars and rumors of wars and nation fighting nation
- Famines, pestilence, earthquakes would happen
- His disciples would be persecuted
- False prophets would come
- They would see Him coming in judgment to Jerusalem

Did all these things occur before AD70?

SECTION TWO
CHAPTER 6
WHEN DID THE CHURCH BEGIN

Dispensationalists teach there is little or no continuity between the Israel of the Old Testament and the New Testament. God has two distinct people - Israel, and the Church.

They teach that the Old Testament saints are not a part of the "church" and are therefore treated differently from those of us who have been saved since the Lord's crucifixion. This terrible and false teaching will lead to a complete misunderstanding of who God's people are and have always been. Please understand this is not those who are physically born as Israelites or national Jews, but it is those who have been true followers of God regardless of whether they are Jew or Gentile.

Those who believe the rapture or removal of all Christians before The Great Tribulation have to distinguish between Israel and the church in order to support their teaching but in doing so they show that they do not understand the nature of Israel and the true church. The New Testament church did not replace the Old Testament church; it fulfills it. Therefore, it is wrong to actually say that the church replaced[37] Israel. The New

---

[37] See Glossary for "Replacement Theology"

Testament church is the Old Testament church being fulfilled or fully developed and this will be completed at the second coming of Christ.

Main Point: God has one church and one plan of salvation through faith and the blood (sacrifice) of Christ, not two churches and two plans of salvation as the dispensationalists try to teach.

You might ask: Why is it important to know who the true church is in order to understand the second coming? While the reasons for understanding the church will not be fully answered here, before we finish this chapter you will see how vital that knowledge is to understanding Christ's coming for all believers, not just the New Testament church as the dispensationalists teach. Suffice it for now that we remember Christ loved the church so much that He died for it and that's the main reason for His second coming.

Another reason for understanding the church for whom Christ is coming is to offset the prominent view of PTDs teaching that Christ has two churches, one in the Old Testament and one in the New Testament. Both of these churches have different ways of being saved, redeemed, or prepared for heaven. This false teaching will be exposed more and more as you read this book.

In order to define and clarify what the true church is, we must answer three questions.

What is the church?

When did the church begin?

When will the church be made perfect?

What Is The Church?

When we refer to the church, we are not referring to a physical building or temple, but to a unique people. In the Bible, the Greek word for church is "ecclesia" which means the called out ones. That means the true church are those people who have been "called out by God" to live in a manner that is pleasing to Him. All people are called by God, but not everyone responds to this call. The true spiritual church are those people from all nations who respond positively by yielding their lives to God. These are people who have repented of their sins, live by faith in Jesus Christ and who follow His teaching. They are different in that they are allowing God to change them into the people He wants them to be, so that when He returns to get them they will be prepared to be permanently united with Him at His second coming. These people are called by various names such as Christians, believers, followers of Christ, the Bride of Christ, His body, but the most important point is that it is these followers of Christ who are God's primary reason for returning to this earth at the second coming or what some call His re-entry.

This church exists as a <u>visible</u> and an <u>invisible</u> entity. That means when you go into a local church assembly where God's people are worshipping you will visibly see people present, but all of them may not be true believers. Therefore, it is important to remember that the visible church may consist of those who are spiritual and those who are not. We cannot always tell the difference because we can't see or judge people's hearts. However, the true or invisible church are those who are following Christ's teachings and thereby prove they trust Him as their Savior.

In the Old Testament, Israel as a nation was the visible church, which was made up of true followers (the spiritual), and those who did not follow Christ (the non-spiritual).

Israel as a nation (visible church) was entrusted with God's revelation which we call the Old Testament.

Romans 3:2b (NIV)

[2]*"First of all, the Jews have been entrusted with the very words of God."*

Put more clearly, God chose Israel or the Jewish nation to be the place where He deposited His truth, trusting they would share that truth with others outside the nation of Israel so they could be blessed by God and become true spiritual followers of Christ. God wanted all people to respond to His invitation to follow His teachings so they would be spiritually reborn and conformed to His image and likeness. God gave Israel not only the Old Testament Scriptures, but God gave Israel Abraham to serve as their national and spiritual father. Abraham modeled how to live by faith and he looked forward to the first coming of Christ and eventually a "heavenly Jerusalem".

Israel as a nation, however, became proud and lost sight of their spiritual calling and purpose and did what some people do today, even in the church. They began to believe that they were spiritual because they were born a Jew rather than a Gentile. Not all Israelites lost sight of their spiritual calling and the need to be obedient and live by faith. No, even in the nation of Israel there was a remnant, a small number of faithful Israelites. These were the true spiritual Israelites. Just as in a visible church, there are some true spiritual followers of Christ and some who are not.

When Christ came to fulfill all the promises and prophecies given to Israel as a nation, the national leaders who should have been spiritual and recognized Him as God's Son, rejected Him because they had lost the message that the true Israel was not the national or political Israel, but the spiritual Israel.

John the Baptist, the forerunner who prepared the way for Christ, tried to get the leaders of Israel (called the Pharisees and Sadducees) to see they were not the true spiritual followers of Abraham who lived by faith but that they were counting on their birth and heritage to save them. Therefore, John the Baptist warns them:

Luke 3:8 (NIV)

[8]"Produce fruit in keeping with repentance. And do not begin to say to yourselves, 'We have Abraham as our father.' For I tell you that out of these stones God can raise up children for Abraham."

Jesus also had to remind the Jewish leaders who were proud of their heritage that they were going to lose their privilege of being God's instrument to bless the world with His salvation message and God was going to take that privilege away and give it to another group of people made up of many nations.

Luke 13:28-29 (NIV)

[28]"There will be weeping there, and gnashing of teeth, when you see Abraham, Isaac and Jacob and all the prophets in the kingdom of God, but you yourselves thrown out. [29]People will come from east and west and north and south, and will take their places at the feast in the kingdom of God."

When this would happen, they would know and others would know because God would allow the symbol of their spiritual privilege and national greatness to be destroyed. That symbol was the temple where God dwelt at one time. Because they refused to live Godly and to share the spiritual message entrusted to them, they would soon no longer be the "apple of God's eye" and God would choose a new church made up of people from all nations to carry on His work.

This did not mean that God's word or promises had failed because God was still going to use spiritual followers to do His work. This is what Paul says:

Romans 9:6-8 (NIV)

⁶"It is not as though God's word had failed. For not all who are descended from Israel are Israel. ⁷Nor because they are his descendants are they all Abraham's children. On the contrary, "It is through Isaac that your offspring will be reckoned." ⁸In other words, it is not the children by physical descent who are God's children, but it is the children of the promise who are regarded as Abraham's offspring."

When Did The Church Begin?

The first members of the spiritual church were the first people to live by faith and accept God's means of salvation through the sacrifice of another. That meant that someone else who was innocent had to pay the price for our redemption or forgiveness. God chose to do this through a blood sacrifice and, therefore, He instituted the animal sacrificial system in the Old Testament to remind us that we cannot save ourselves and that our sins hurt the innocent. Every time Old Testament followers of Christ offered the prescribed blood sacrifice as a payment for their sins, they were doing the following: First, they were saying, I need someone to save me, as I cannot save myself. Secondly, they were saying that the sacrifice pointed to a sinless Messiah who would someday come and die once and for all for the sins of God's people. Thirdly, they were obeying God by offering the right sacrifice with a repentant heart. That is why in Hebrews 9:22 the Bible says: "without the shedding of blood there is no forgiveness of sin".

Now, back to the question: Who were the first persons to ever be saved and the answer is Adam and Eve because after they sinned in the Garden of Eden, God clothed their nakedness (a type of their shame) with animal skins.

Genesis 3:21 (NIV)

21 "*The LORD God made garments of skin for Adam and his wife and clothed them.*"

We are not told in this verse what animals were skinned and died in order to cover Adam and Eve, but we are indirectly told in the story of Cain and Abel in chapter 4. No doubt Adam and Eve taught their children God's requirement for a "blood sacrifice" and that He would accept no other as it pointed to and represented Christ on the cross and that we are not saved by what we do, but by what He did, so there is no boasting. Let's look at Cain and Abel who both brought sacrifices to God, but only one was accepted because Abel obeyed and followed God's direction.

Genesis 4:1-4 (NIV)

[1]"Adam made love to his wife Eve, and she became pregnant and gave birth to Cain. She said, "With the help of the LORD I have brought forth a man." [2]Later she gave birth to his brother Abel. Now Abel kept flocks, and Cain worked the soil. [3]In the course of time, Cain brought some of the fruits of the soil as an offering to the LORD. [4]And Abel also brought an offering—fat portions from some of the firstborn of his flock. The LORD looked with favor on Abel and his offering...."

Why was Abel's sacrifice acceptable to God and Cain's was not? The answer was because Abel followed God's command to bring a "lamb" or blood sacrifice instead of a bloodless sacrifice. Remember, true believers are followers of God and that means they obey His commands, even when they don't fully understand them.

Every person who offered a blood sacrifice in the Old Testament with a repentant heart was a true spiritual believer who was confessing he needed a Savior and was looking to Christ's death, which had not yet occurred. The spiritual Israelites looked forward to the cross, which was the perfect blood sacrifice, and we look backward to the cross, but no one has ever been redeemed or forgiven, either in the Old Testament or the New Testament except by faith in Christ. It is true they did not have the full revelation or understanding that we do of who and what Christ was going to do, but they were faithful to follow the Lord by humbly trusting in God's means of salvation, not their own good works. It is the same with us today. We are saved by faith in what Christ did for us as they were saved by faith in what He would do for them. All Israelites who humbly acknowledged and repented of their sins and trusted in the sacrifices that pointed to Christ were the true spiritual Israelites. Again, the true church of the Old Testament was not national but spiritual and they were saved by looking to the cross and we are saved by looking back to the cross.

So the answer to "When did the church begin?" is it began with the first person who by faith trusted God and proved it by putting his faith in God's means of atonement—the blood of Christ.

Those who looked forward to the cross and those who look back to the cross are in the same church. These are the people for whom Christ comes at His second coming. Christ is not the shepherd of two flocks, but one "flock" made up of both Old and New Testament followers of Christ. There is only one coming of Christ for His church and only one time when He takes all of His children back to heaven. To teach that the Lord treats the Old Testament saints different is simply a serious and erroneous misapplication of the Bible.

John 10:16 (NIV)

16"I have other sheep that are not of this sheep pen. I must bring them also. They too will listen to my voice, and there shall be one flock and one shepherd."

When Will The Church (true believers) Be Made Perfect?

Presently we are being conformed to the image of God and conditioned for heaven by learning more and more about Christ through the Scriptures and by bringing our lives into conformity with God's Word. This requires that we are humble, willing to confess our sins and repent of them in an on-going fashion. Also, we are being made perfect by the things that we suffer, but we will not be made whole or perfect until Christ comes back and transforms our body, soul and spirit. We are in process and we need to keep praying for each other as Paul prayed for us:

I Thessalonians 5:23 (NIV)

23"May God himself, the God of peace, sanctify you through and through. May your whole spirit, soul and body be kept blameless at the coming of our Lord Jesus Christ."

This being made perfect in the Bible is called "sanctification" which is the process by which the Holy Spirit uses to conform and morph us into Christ-likeness.

Please note that process in our previous text is not completed until the second coming of Christ.

Conclusion

The church is made up of the true followers of Christ from both the Old Testament all the way to the present. There are not two "flocks" and two plans of salvation. Every person from the beginning of Genesis is saved by faith—a faith that is manifested in obedience to God.

This is important because those who teach the church is different from Israel do so by not distinguishing between the true Israel and the visible Israel. The church was conceived in the Old Testament and was born on the day of Pentecost and received its body. But it will not be fully matured and made perfect until Christ comes. God has fulfilled all His promises to the nation of Israel and is fulfilling all His promises to spiritual Israel in and through the church which exists as Old and New Testament saints. It is our responsibility to spread the Gospel to the whole world.

One More Thing

I want to address one more thing regarding the church. It is, without doubt, a serious issue and that is what we see as a cult[38]. If the religious group, denomination, or organization is teaching a doctrinal

---

[38] See Glossary definition of a cult

belief that seems to not follow what Orthodox Christians[39] believe, then it is a cult by definition. Look at what Paul says to the church at Galatia.

Galatians 1:8 (NIV)

[8]But even if we or an angel from heaven should preach a gospel other than the one we preached to you, let them be under God's curse!

A false teaching by cults is they do not accept Jesus Christ as God, the second person of the Trinity. They sometimes will refer to Him as "a" god. Jehovah's Witnesses[40] are famous for that one. Mormons[41] do not believe in the Trinity as we understand it. They believe that God and Jesus were separate physical people who dwelt on the earth. They say God was Jesus' physical father, and both men died. They believe the Bible to be the Word of God as far as it is translated correctly (by them), and they also believe the Book of Mormon[42] to be a more accurate revelation from God. In case of any conflict between the Bible and the Book of Mormon, the Book of Mormon is correct. They also believe in works as a part of your salvation. If you wish to study the cults further, I highly recommend the book *"The Kingdom of the Cults"* by Walter Martin.

---

[39] ibid Orthodox Christian
[40] See Glossary for the definition of Jehovah's Witnesses
[41] See Glossary for the definition of Mormons
[42] See Glossary for "book of Mormon"

Review

1. If the Old Testament saints or followers of Christ are not a part of the New Testament church but are a Jewish church as dispensationalists teach, then when is the Old Testament church or saints to be raptured or lifted out?

2. Does the Bible teach two plans or means of salvation: one for the Jew and one for the Christian?

3. What is the difference between the visible church and the true church?

4. Does the Bible teach there are two "flocks" or "one flock"?

5. Will the Old Testament saints be resurrected with the New Testament saints or at a separate time?

CHAPTER 7
DON'T GO BACKWARDS

Background:

The Book of Hebrews is named properly. The book was primarily written to Jewish (Hebrew) Christians, some of whom had recently been converted to Christianity. The book was written, in this author's opinion, by the Apostle Paul and was likely translated into Greek by Luke or Apollos.[43]

Imagine it is AD61-AD63, seven years before the destruction of the temple in Jerusalem, which was a holocaust against the nation of Israel. Many of the Christians converts on the Day of Pentecost were persecuted by the Jews in Jerusalem because a large number of those Jews who were converted to Christianity (Acts 2) had fled to Rome after leaving Judaism for Christ. While in Rome they avoided the seven Jewish synagogues in Rome, perhaps for fear of more persecution.

Somewhere between AD61 and AD63, the apostle Paul was led of the Lord to go to Rome to share the Gospel with the leaders of the Jewish synagogues. Paul was well qualified to do this as he had been converted from being a Jewish scholar to being a Christian apostle while on the road to Damascus. Upon arrival at Rome,

---

[43] I am convinced that Paul wrote the Book of Hebrews even though there are others who think he didn't.
See Glossary for who Apollos was.

Paul invited the Jewish synagogue rulers to dialogue with Him concerning Christ and many of them turned to Christ as new believers (Acts 28:24). Paul then left to go to Spain to preach but was to return to Rome to meet with Peter.

While Paul was in Spain, the Roman Emperor Nero in July AD64 set the city of Rome on fire and blamed the Christians. In his deranged mind, he accused Christians of being anti-Roman, accusing them of being cannibals by misrepresenting the Eucharist meal in an attempt to justify his persecution of Christians. His torture of Christians by October AD64 included feeding them to wild animals, covering them in flammable material and securing them to stakes and burning them as human torches.

The new Jewish converts to Christianity were not targeted because they were still associated with the synagogues and considered Jews. This allowed the new Jewish converts to minister to the older, more mature Christians, and most likely Peter himself. We are not sure when Paul had gotten back to Rome to meet with Peter before he was killed by Nero, but most likely he had returned. Then Nero killed Peter by crucifying him and according to tradition he was crucified upside down at his own request. With one of the primary apostles killed, some of the new Jewish Christians began to waver and considered returning to Judaism because of the persecution and the very fact they had not yet been taught about the superiority of Christianity over the Old Covenant of Judaism.

Perhaps when Paul heard of the temptation and the leanings of this new group that was considering returning to Judaism with all of its sacrifices, this was when he wrote the Book of Hebrews. The Book of Hebrews was written to this group of believers who had not yet departed from the faith to persuade them that a return to Judaism would be a form of apostasy or falling away from the faith and that to do so would make the sacrifice of Christ for them to be of no avail.

The urgency of their need to understand the superiority of Christ's sacrifice and the sacrifices of the temple, which were "shadows", "signs", and "pictures" of the real sacrifice of Christ most likely expedited Paul's return to Rome, if he had not yet returned, and where he was also put to death by Nero.

Time will not allow us to cover all the material in Hebrews so I am going to focus our attention on the five warning sections of Hebrews. Before doing so, it is necessary to remind you again that the purpose of the book of Hebrews was to show the Jewish Christians the superiority of Christ. It is the magnum opus[44] written under divine inspiration to prevent converted Christian Jews from returning to Judaism, which would be a form of apostasy or falling away from the true faith.

---

[44] See Glossary for "magnum opus"

The First Warning

To return to the Old Testament sacrifices would be a form of "crucifying Christ afresh and anew" and rejecting His supreme sacrifice or atonement for their sin, leaving them "unforgiven" and without salvation. Please read the following Scriptures.

Hebrews 6:1-6 (NIV)

¹Therefore let us move beyond the elementary teachings about Christ and be taken forward to maturity, not laying again the foundation of repentance from acts that lead to death, and of faith in God, ²instruction about cleansing rites, the laying on of hands, the resurrection of the dead, and eternal judgment.³And God permitting, we will do so ⁴It is impossible for those who have once been enlightened, who have tasted the heavenly gift, who have shared in the Holy Spirit, ⁵who have tasted the goodness of the word of God and the powers of the coming age ⁶and who have fallen away, to be brought back to repentance. To their loss they are crucifying the Son of God all over again and subjecting him to public disgrace.

Hebrews 10:24-29 (NIV)

[24]And let us consider how we may spur one another on toward love and good deeds, [25]not giving up meeting together, as some are in the habit of doing, but encouraging one another—and all the more as you see the Day approaching [26]If we deliberately keep on sinning after we have received the knowledge of the truth, no sacrifice for sins is left, [27]but only a fearful expectation of judgment and of raging fire that will consume the enemies of God. [28]Anyone who rejected the law of Moses died without mercy on the testimony of two or three witnesses. [29]How much more severely do you think someone deserves to be punished who has trampled the Son of God underfoot, who has treated as an unholy thing the blood of the covenant that sanctified them, and who has insulted the Spirit of grace?"

The Second Warning

To turn back and reject the fact that Christ "died once for all" (Hebrews 9:28; I Peter 3:18) for our sins and to deny He tasted death for all men (Hebrews 2:9) is to fail to escape God's judgment.

Hebrews 2:1-4 (NIV)

¹We must pay the most careful attention, therefore, to what we have heard, so that we do not drift away. ²For since the message spoken through angels was binding, and every violation and disobedience received it's just punishment, ³ how shall we escape if we ignore so great a_salvation? This salvation, which was first announced by the Lord, was confirmed to us by those who heard him.⁴God also testified to it by signs, wonders and various miracles, and by gifts of the Holy Spirit distributed according to his will.

For the Christian Jew to turn back to Judaism is to "fall short" and fail to enter into the rest of eternal life.

Hebrews 4:1-3 (NIV)

¹Therefore, since the promise of entering his rest still stands, let us be careful that none of you be found to have fallen short of it. ²For we also have had the good news proclaimed to us, just as they did; but the message they heard was of no value to them [the unbelieving Jews], because they did not share the faith of those who obeyed. ³Now we who have believed enter that rest, just as God has said, "So I declared on oath in my anger, 'They shall never enter my rest.'" And yet his works have been finished since the creation of the world.
[brackets are inserted by the authors of this book].

The Old Testament sacrifices were types or signs that pointed to Christ who is the real sacrifice. To go back to Judaism is to regress to the signs, shadows, and types at the expense of the real. Again, let me use an analogy: As I travel south I become hungry. I see a road sign that says there is a famous restaurant ahead at the next exit. On that sign is a picture of some of their delicious food. I take the exit, I eat and taste of this marvelous food, and find it very satisfying. Now, do I go back every time I am hungry and read the sign or eat the sign? No! Why would I settle for the sign when I have the real meal? To go back to Judaism or to mix Judaism with our new standing with Christ is to return to sign reading or as Galatians says: the "weak and miserable forces".

Galatians 4:8-11 (NIV)

[8]Formerly, when you did not know God, you were slaves to those who by nature are not gods. [9]But now that you know God—or rather are known by God—how is it that you are turning back to those weak and miserable forces? Do you wish to be enslaved by them all over again? [10]You are observing special days and months and seasons and years! [11]I fear for you, that somehow I have wasted my efforts on you.

The Third Warning

The Greek word for "weak and miserable" in Galatians is *"ptochos"* and carries with it the idea of a beggar who begs for alms or help. The purpose of the Old Testament Law was to show us our destitute state so that we would look to God. All the old sacrifices were types that pointed us to Christ, so that we would trust Him, instead of our own so-called good works. All our works are as filthy rags because they fall short of God's holy laws that reflect God's holy nature. The law did not save and could not save us; it only revealed our sinfulness, so that we would throw ourselves on the mercy of God.

Romans 7:7 (NIV)

⁷What shall we say, then? Is the law sinful? Certainly not! Nevertheless, I would not have known what sin was had it not been for the law. For I would not have known what coveting really was if the law had not said, "You shall not covet."

In order to understand why Galatians says that the Old Covenant with all its rituals and laws are weak, one must understand what the law could and could not do. The law could not save you as it only told you God's absolute standard for you which was perfection. The law was to reveal how far short of the revealed will of God we had fallen.

Perhaps an illustration will help. When I was growing up we had a glass carafe in the refrigerator to keep the drinking water cool. The rule of the house was that when you were thirsty you did not drink out of the carafe, but you poured it into a glass and you refilled the carafe when you were finished. On at least one occasion, after eating crackers, I was thirsty and drank out of the carafe. Later my mother took the carafe from the refrigerator and shook it and saw all the cracker crumbs floating in the carafe. I was confronted with her holding the carafe and accusing me of drinking out of the carafe. The evidence of my offense was apparent. That is what the absolute, pure, spiritual law of God does: It shakes us up and shows us how "crummy" we are and our need of God's mercy. How many of you have ever had a police officer give you a ticket for speeding and then have the officer offer to pay your ticket? I would bet never because the law does not save you by paying the ticket. Christ who perfectly kept the law paid the fine for us. Again, notice that Romans 7:7 says that *"I would not have known what sin was had it not been for the law."*

The Fourth Warning

To go back to Judaism is to reject the payment for our sins by Christ's sacrifice and return to trying to keep the law, which leads us to slavery and leaves us without any hope of help. If we refuse the only help that God has provided, which is the sacrifice of His only Son, the old sacrifices won't save us. There is no spiritual soul rest in doing that and there is no eternal rest (heaven) if we return to Judaism. For anyone, but especially the Christian Jews to return to the law, the temple sacrifices and/or Judaism would be to reject the sacrificial payment of Christ and would again place us under the curse of the law and imprison us in legalism. It would then take the place of grace by returning us to the law which Christ did away with on the cross.

The Fifth Warning

The last warning we want to illustrate here about going back to Judaism comes in Hebrews 5:1-12. The writer warns two groups, those who are weak (new Jewish converts) and those who are wicked (5:11-6:3). However, those who are weak ought not to be weak. They knew the Old Testament and all about

Melchizedek.[45] Jesus was ordained of God to be the High Priest after the order of Melchizedek, not Aaron.[46] Christ is the final and ultimate High Priest. Christ is the Great High Priest who offered Himself as the supreme sacrifice, once for all.

However, Paul pauses and basically says, "I would like to dialogue with you about the greatness of Christ's priesthood, but you are too immature and child-like to listen. Your desire for ritualism has fostered spiritual deafness." Paul uses this language because he is reminding them that the Old Testament revelation was not complete or full and was geared for those who lived in the infancy stage of Christianity. It was time for them to move on from the shadows, rituals and teachings of the Old Testament into maturity that comes through Christ fulfilling the Old Testament.

Hebrews 5:10-12 (NIV)

[10]...And was designated by God to be high priest in the order of Melchizedek.[11]We have much to say about this, but it is hard to make it clear to you because you no longer try to understand. [12]In fact, though by this time you ought to be teachers, you need someone to teach you the elementary truths of God's word all over again. You need milk, not solid food!

---

[45] See Glossary for description of Melchizedek
[46] Ibid for Aaron

Further, Paul goes on to tell the Hebrew Christians that the Old Covenant is fulfilled in the New Covenant thus making the Old "obsolete". The Greek word for "obsolete" gives the word picture of a worn-out old garment that is declared no longer usable or needed.

Hebrews 8:13 (NIV)

[13]By calling this covenant 'new', he has made the first one obsolete; and what is obsolete and outdated will soon disappear.

If it is asked why I took such time on the Book of Hebrews in regard to the second coming, it is because it doesn't support any teaching about renewed sacrifices. The old covenant has been made obsolete. It is critical that we understand this false doctrine. At the risk of appearing repetitious, some of my dear brothers and sisters in Christ who are dispensationalists, pre-millennial, pre-tribulation rapture advocates (PTDs)[47] are teaching that the temple will be rebuilt during what they call the seven-year tribulation and that the temple will be not only present as a memorial during the millennium or 1000-year reign of Christ mentioned in Revelation 20, but the Jews will practice again the offering of sacrifices for the atonement of sin. That to me and my co-author undermines the atoning work of Christ and borders on a most serious false doctrinal teaching according to Hebrews. Please read what LaHaye wrote and consider

---

[47] See Glossary for PTDs

what we have learned from Hebrews. Review his quotes to understand our concern of this very false and dangerous teaching. Unless I am missing something here, it is quite evident that there is no more sacrifice for sin, period. To me, this comes very close to heresy. Either Christ died once for all or His sacrifice on the cross was for some but not others. His death and resurrection was a complete covering for all of our sins, including the Jewish believers, or it was only a partial sacrifice for some but not others.

Drs. Tim LaHaye and Ice in their book *Clarifying the End Times write the following:*

"The Bible speaks of four Temples in Jerusalem. The first two, Solomon and Herod's, have already been built and destroyed. The final two, the Tribulation Temple and the Millennial Temple, have yet to be built and are described in great detail in biblical prophecy. In the eternal state, there will be no Temple because the new heaven and new earth are not polluted with sin, and God who is holy, will be able to dwell openly with man."

Then Dr. LaHaye quotes Jerry Hullinger to underscore the point:

"Because of God's promise to dwell on earth during the millennium (as stated in the New Covenant), it is necessary that he protect his presence through sacrifice...During the eternal state, all inhabitants of the New Jerusalem will be glorified and will therefore not be a source of contagious impurities to defile the holiness of God." [48]

The Bible does not speak of a third and fourth temple but it is merely again an assumption on LaHaye and others' opinions. I find no hint, much less great detail, of either a tribulation temple or a millennial temple. It is very interesting to me that the PTDs can get so much out of nothing. The temple and its sacrificial practices are over. When the veil[49] was torn in two at the Lord's crucifixion, God declared the temple sacrifices done. Jesus became our high priest and we are now able to go directly to the Holy of Holies through the one and only high priest.

When I first heard about LaHaye and other PTDs teaching this doctrine, I rejected it because it seemed so absurd and I really felt this was a misunderstanding by the person who related it to me. It was only after I read some of LaHaye's writings that I realized he really believes in the renewal of daily sacrifices and two more rebuilt temples. Of all the false teachings by the PTDs, this is one of the most dangerous and wrong. It looks like LaHaye and his followers are going backward. What a shame! As for the writers of this book, we clearly stand opposed to such an erroneous misunderstanding of God's Word.

---

[48] LaHaye and Ice, Clarifying the End Times, pg. 94-95
[49] See Glossary for a description of the veil

SECTION THREE

CHAPTER 8

INTRODUCTION TO

UNDERSTANDING REVELATION

In this book, up until now, we have endeavored to make the material as understandable as possible. We have covered enough information that if you are truly searching for the truth about eschatology, it really isn't necessary for any more to be said. However, with the popularity of the discussion of Revelation in today's world, we would be remiss if we didn't address the book at least to some degree.

Proper exegesis[50] of end-times prophecy is to understand Revelation in light of all other prophecies, not the other way around. Many people have told me that Revelation is hard to understand and I agree with that if you start with Revelation first and then try to fit other prophetic writings into it.

In review, we have clearly shown there is no rapture or lifting out of Christians prior to the Lord's visible and final return. The Christians will continue to be here with the unsaved until the end based on several passages of Scripture in both the Old and New Testament.

---

[50] See Glossary for the definition of exegesis

We have debunked the idea of a seven-year period of "great tribulation" as something that is yet to come in the future. As a reminder, there is no seven-year period which the world has yet to go through with great duress. History shows us that Jerusalem suffered greatly during the first-century siege of the Romans as a judgment by God during the period shortly before the temple was destroyed in AD70. Historical evidence recorded by the Jewish historian Josephus makes it abundantly clear that Nero was the first emperor to persecute believers, which lasted for 42 months almost to the day, and is mentioned in Scripture.

We have addressed the issue of a 1000-year reign on this earth by our Lord and He Himself tried to make it obvious that His reign was not of this earth, but is a heavenly Lordship. I find it amazing that as the Jews were looking for an earthly Messiah, and the disciples were looking for an earthly king, that we still have many people, both Jews, and Christians, who are still believing there will be an earthly Messiah/Savior ruler in the future.

We have addressed many other pertinent issues that are important in the study of last-days prophetical studies in the earlier chapters of this book, but will need to give, at least, an overview of Revelation. There is no way this section can be a complete dissertation and study of Revelation, but we will simply be addressing the most important or most discussed writings by John in this book.

This section has been left until near the end as it

really is somewhat more difficult to comprehend and is not totally necessary, although very interesting, for the understanding and importance of end-times prophecy. Granted, it certainly has an impact on the overall study, but is not absolutely necessary in receiving the truth and impact of eschatology. Due to the somewhat deep and symbolical writing of Revelation, it can be easily misunderstood and taken to mean something other than what I believe was intended. We need to understand that John is revealing (Revelation) information mainly to the seven churches and, for the most part, we are just bystanders. Do you honestly think that God directed John to write mysteriously in such a way that only 20th century readers could understand it? Or do you think maybe John wrote in such a way so that the first century church understood it clearly? Which may be the better option here?

Having said that, I trust that as you enter this section you will find the information helpful, enjoyable and enlightening as you study the contents.

Remember, John is writing to the seven churches addressed in his opening statement. The book is clearly intended for them to understand, even though there is a lot of symbolism in it. Much Hebrew writing was written in this manner. More than two-thirds of the writings in Revelation reference the Old Testament in some form or another. I do want to briefly address some issues and hopefully clear up some confusion for your understanding before moving into the next chapters that Pastor Dan has spent his time and knowledge in an effort to share with us.

My first one is concerning the identity and mark of the beast in Revelation chapter 13.

The Beast Of Revelation
Revelation 13:18 (NIV)

18This calls for wisdom. Let the person who has insight calculate the number of the beast, for it is the number of a man. That number is 666.

I had initially planned on writing an entire chapter on the subject of who the beast is or was but found that it would be best to look at what others have written and I believe that it is not necessary for me to spend a lengthy amount of time researching and writing this chapter.

Across the years one of the most popular topics concerning end-times prophecy has been who the beast is that John wrote about in Revelation chapter 13 and identifying him with the number 666.

There have been many men who have been accused of being the beast, but there is only one who can be clearly and completely identified from the description found in Revelation. They include many popular men in history as well as political leaders. It is undoubtedly one of the most controversial topics of the day regarding end-times prophecy. After all options are examined, Nero is the only one that fits the "Beast of Revelation" description completely.

I could take a lot of time and write much on the identification of who he is and how the number 666 identifies him, but there has been a lot of credible research already done by others, especially Dr. Kenneth Gentry. His book titled *"The Beast of Revelation"* gives a very good explanation of who this person is. So at this point, I will defer presenting most of this information in light of the fact that Dr. Gentry has done a much better job than I could have done in presenting this material.

I will just simply tell you that John points the finger directly at Nero Caesar. Dr. Gentry identifies him: "The Beast of Revelation in his incarnation is none other than the infamous Lucius Domitius Ahenobarbus. Though you probably don't know him by his birth name, you certainly will recognize his adoptive name: Nero Claudius Caesar."[51] In the next several chapters of his book, Dr. Gentry explains how this is true. He addresses not only his identity but also his character, his war, his worship and other pertinent information.

---

[51] The Beast of Revelation, Dr. Kenneth L. Gentry (American Vision, Powder Springs Georgia 2002) Page 13

The Persecution And Evilness Of Nero To Christians

"Nero's persecution, which was initiated in AD64, was the first ever Roman assault on Christianity. Roman historian *Tacitus* (AD56-AD117) spoke of Nero's "cruel nature" that "put to death so many innocent men".[52] He records the scene in Rome when the persecution of Christians broke out: "And their death was aggravated with mockeries, insomuch that, wrapped in the hides of wild beasts, they were torn to pieces by dogs, or fastened to crosses to be set on fire, that when the darkness fell they might be burned to illuminate the night".[53] "Christians were crucified, beheaded, burnt alive, and used as torches to light the palace gardens. Historically, Nero is the one that persecuted Christians beyond all comparison. St. John's banishment to Patmos (where he wrote the book of Apocalypse) was itself a result of the great persecution of Nero. The apostle Paul was tortured and then beheaded by the evil Emperor Nero at Rome in AD67. The apostle Peter, who was crucified upside down, was another victim of Nero."[54]

---

[52] The Book of Revelation Made Easy by Dr. Kenneth L. Gentry (American Vision, Powder Springs Georgia 2008) Page 59

[53] Copied from Ecclesia.org, "The mark of the Beast" by Richard Anthony

[54] The mystery of 666 Explained - Nero! 2009 | Richard Anthony. ecclesia.org/truth/beast.html

Nero's Supposed Deity And Worship

Nero was convinced that he was the new or reincarnated "Apollo" and had many of the same attributes. Other famous people of the day lifted Nero up as a god such as Seneca who was Nero's tutor and convinced him that he was a god. Suetonius was another recognized leader who promoted Nero as a god.

Nero's portrait appears on some coins as Apollo playing his lyre. He had a huge statue erected in the temple of Mars in Rome. It was the same size as the one of Mars, himself.

Dr. Gentry writes "Nero was actually worshiped, for inscriptions found in Ephesus call him "Almighty God" and "Savior". Nero is referred to as "God and Savior" in an inscription at Salamis, Cyprus."[55]   Dr. Gentry also writes, "For those who expect the beast to appear on the scene of history at any moment, another surprise awaits. The material in Revelation is quite clear: The beast has already intruded upon the scene of history in our distant past."[56]

This argument is quite compelling given the fact that John was writing to his contemporaries and not to those of us 2000 years or more later. Why would the first century believers read this with the understanding of who

---

[55] Gentry, The Beast of Revelation (American Vision, Powder Springs, Georgia, 2002) Page 81
[56] ibid Page 7

the beast was if he were not to be identified until centuries down the road. I believe that is why the Holy Spirit was so specific in directing John to write such an understandable symbolic description of both the city or general area where the beast resided as well as the identity of the beast by using a number that could easily point to Nero. Dr. Gentry writes: "I must note a widely recognized problem regarding the Beast imagery. Most commentators agree that the beast in Revelation shifts between the generic and the specific. That is, sometimes the beast pictures a kingdom, sometimes a particular individual leader of that kingdom."[57]

Revelation 17:9 (NIV)

[9]This calls for a mind with wisdom. The seven heads are seven hills on which the woman sits.

This passage easily fits with the understanding that John is identifying the beast in terms of location and that Rome was the place where the "man" resided. The "generic" is based on his residence and the "specific" identifies the man himself. To identify anyone else requires a great deal of assuming in the writings of Revelation as well as misapplication of other passages.

---

[57] Ibid Page 10

Revelation 17:10 (NIV)

¹⁰They are also seven kings. Five have fallen, one is, the other has not yet come; but when he does come, he must remain for only a little while.

In this passage John has placed the position of the beast in the ruling lineage of Rome and where he fits by saying that he is the sixth king with only one more to come for a short time. Here is a list of the seven kings John is writing about:

"Five have fallen..." **1**. Julius Caesar (49-44BC) **2**. Augustus (27BC-AD 14) **3**. Tiberius (AD14-37) **4**. Caligula (AD37-41) **5**. Claudius (AD41-54) *"One is..."* **6**. Nero (AD54-68) *"the other has not yet come; but when he does come, he must remain for only a little while."*[58] **7**. Galba (June AD68-January AD69, a six-month ruler-ship) Of the first seven kings of the Roman Empire, five had come (Julius Caesar, Augustus, Tiberius, Gaius, and Claudius), one was now in power (Nero), and one had not yet come (Galba), but would only remain a little time (six months).[59]

The Mark of the Beast

The mark of the beast just adds to the speculation of who he was or is and the significant impact of his power on mankind.

---

[58] Bold, Italics quotes are taken directly from Revelation 17:10
[59] Ken Gentry, The Beast of Revelation, American Vision Press, Powder Springs GA. Lineage of the seven Caesars compiled from pages 138 through 145

Revelation 13: 16,17 (NIV)

16It also forced all people, great and small, rich and poor, free and slave, to receive a mark on their right hands or on their foreheads, 17so that they could not buy or sell unless they had the mark, which is the name of the beast or the number of its name.

First of all, may I share with you what the mark is not. (1) It is not a microchip or any type of electronic implantation. (2) It is not a credit card or anything related to that type of device. (3) It is not your social security card or a number that identifies you personally. (4) In fact, it is not anything electronic or physical that the early church could not be able to identify, but like much of Revelation, it is a form of symbolism that represents a deeper meaning.

The idea that we will be implanted with a microchip or some device like that is just simply ludicrous and certainly no one would understand such an explanation in the first-century church. The first-century church would not be able to understand credit cards or social security numbers either. But, given the idea that I share below, the early church would have clearly understood the significance of a mark on the forehead or on the hand and what it meant.

Realizing that most of Revelation is symbolism, I began to look at other places in the Bible to see if there were more references to the idea of a symbolic mark on the hand or the forehead and what the inferred meaning might be. When I found this one in Exodus 13:9, I began to understand how it might pertain to what John wrote in Revelation regarding the mark of the beast. I was taught in Bible College to use other Scriptures to clarify a particular passage if it needed clarification. Also, we were taught that whenever possible, we should apply "the law of first mention". This simply means that wherever the reference is first seen in Scripture, it should take on a more meaningful role in the total understanding of the subject matter being studied. With that in mind, I began to take a deeper look at the following passage in Exodus.

Exodus 13:9 (NIV)

⁹This observance will be for you like a sign on your hand and a reminder on your forehead that this law of the LORD is to be on your lips. For the LORD brought you out of Egypt with his mighty hand.

After looking at this passage as well as a couple more found in Deuteronomy 6:8 and 11:18, it became clear to me that God was using this symbolic picture of the mark on the head and hand as meaning that **whatever or whoever controls our mind is what controls what we think and the mark on our hand controls what we do. WOW! It is where our allegiance is.** Please don't overlook this truth. It's our **allegiance**, not a physical mark. There are literally dozens of Scriptures that talk about a "mark", or in some cases a "seal", describing something written on or in us.

Now let's apply this same understanding to the passage found in Revelation regarding the mark. Looking at this next passage should confirm to us that this is not a literal physical mark but a symbol of something deeper.

Revelation 14:1 (NIV)

¹Then I looked, and there before me was the Lamb, standing on Mount Zion and with him 144,000 who had his name and his Father's name written on their foreheads.

Do you honestly think there are or were 144,000 who all had the Lamb's name and the Father's name tattooed on their foreheads? Knowing that most of Revelation is symbolism, wouldn't it be much better to look at these verses with the understanding that the symbols are representative of something else and should not be taken literally as the dispensationalists want to do?

Understanding Revelation 13:16-17

What kind of power would someone or something have to force everyone who would not bow down and worship this beast or image to not be able to buy or sell unless they had the mark? Remember, we have already established the fact that the beast was both generic in nature as well as a specific person. The generic identification was Rome and the specific person was Nero.

With this in mind, did Rome or Nero demand that citizens of that day worship the beast or require a "mark" of identification to buy and sell? Let's take a look at the history.

The Libellus

The Christians of the first century were under the military authority of Rome, a nation which openly proclaimed its rulers, the Caesars, to be divine. All those under the jurisdiction of Rome were required by law to publicly proclaim their allegiance to Caesar by burning a pinch of incense and declaring, "Caesar is Lord". Upon compliance with this law, the people were given a papyrus document called a "libellus", which they were required to present when either stopped by the Roman police or attempting to engage in commerce in the Roman marketplace or Agora, increasing the difficulty of "buying or selling" without this mark. This is the essence of Scripture's warnings to the early Christians against taking upon themselves the **"mark of the beast"**.[60] I recommend that you go to Ecclesia.org and read the entire document by Richard Anthony titled "The mystery of 666 Explained" as well as the article titled "The Mark of the Beast".

---

[60] The mystery of 666 Explained - Nero! 2009 | Richard Anthony. ecclesia.org/truth/beast.html

The Antichrist

The next item I wish to address is the confusion concerning the fact there are those who claim that the beast in Revelation and the so-called antichrist that John wrote about in his epistles are one and the same person. This is simply not the case. I will briefly address some of the issues concerning this mistaken belief. Listed below are the only four references in the entire Bible of the word "antichrist" and all of them are found in 1 and 2 John. Note that John writes about many antichrists as well as the spirit of antichrist.

1 John 2:18-22 (NIV)

18Dear children, this is the last hour; and as you have heard that the antichrist is coming, even now many antichrists have come. This is how we know it is the last hour. 19They went out from us, but they did not really belong to us. For if they had belonged to us, they would have remained with us; but their going showed that none of them belonged to us. 20But you have an anointing from the Holy One, and all of you know the truth. 21I do not write to you because you do not know the truth, but because you do know it and because no lie comes from the truth. 22Who is the liar? It is whoever denies that Jesus is the Christ. Such a person is the antichrist denying the Father and the Son.

138

1 John 4:3 (NIV)

³but every spirit that does not acknowledge Jesus is not from God. This is the spirit of the antichrist, which you have heard is coming and even now is already in the world.

2 John 7 (NIV)

⁷I say this because many deceivers, who do not acknowledge Jesus Christ as coming in the flesh, have gone out into the world. Any such person is the deceiver and the antichrist.

I will only deal with this briefly and explain that the antichrist John is writing about here is not specifically the Beast of Revelation. Granted, certainly Nero was as "antichrist" as you can get, but this term used here by John is a more generic term and intended to mean a group of people who were opposed to the Lord. They were apparently teaching false doctrine and some were believing it. It is important to understand that John was speaking of several people and not just one person called "The Antichrist". This is just another example of the PTDs trying to shoehorn end-times prophecy into their misguided approach by applying a futuristic slant on something that has already taken place.

Gary DeMar writes, "Antichrist is simply any belief system that disputes the fundamental teachings of

Christianity, beginning with the person of Christ. These antichrists are 'religious' figures. The antichrist, contrary to much present-day speculation, is not a political figure, no matter how *anti*-(against) Christ he might be."[61]

This record by John is just simply fulfilling prophecy that Jesus told us about in Matthew 24.

Matthew 24:10-11 (NIV)

[10]At that time, many will turn away from the faith and will betray and hate each other, [11]and many false prophets will appear and deceive many people.

The next item I would like to address is the "man of sin" found in the following passage.

II Thessalonians 2:3-7 (NIV)

[3]Don't let anyone deceive you in any way, for that day will not come until the rebellion occurs and the man of lawlessness is revealed, the man doomed to destruction. [4]He will oppose and will exalt himself over everything that is called God or is worshiped, so that he sets himself up in God's temple, proclaiming himself to be God. [5]Don't you remember that when I was with you I used to tell you these things? [6]And now you know what is holding him back so that he may be revealed at the proper time. [7]For the secret power of lawlessness is

---

[61] Last Days Madness (American Vision, Powder Springs Georgia, 1999) Page 269

already at work, but the one who now holds it back will continue to do so till he is taken out of the way.

This is clearly referring to Nero as the Beast in Revelation. It is interesting to note that up until Nero, the Roman government protected Christians. They even opposed the Jewish leaders from doing anything harmful to the early church. It is also interesting to note that Paul felt the church at Thessalonica already knew who or what was holding back the "man of lawlessness" or "man of sin" (KJV).

There are several theories on who or what is doing the "holding back" but apparently according to verse 6, the church knew. For us, it's merely an idea and, therefore, we aren't sure. We do know that the "man of sin" is the same person as the "Beast of Revelation" which has been identified as Nero. With this being the case, the restrainer could have been the Roman government until the reign of Nero. When Nero came to power, he turned the protection of Christians around and began to persecute them. There are many historical records of this persecution and the devastating treatment of the Roman believers.

This we know regarding the timeline. Paul wrote to the church at Thessalonica in around AD52 before Nero came to power. Nero began the persecution of Christians in AD64.

No Rebuilt Temple In Scripture

Contrary to the popular opinion of dispensationalists, there is not one Scripture that points to a rebuilding of a third or fourth temple unless you first make a lot of assumptions. This is just simply their idea to infer that there will be renewed temple worship and daily sacrifice practiced by the Jews during a seven-year tribulation and a supposed 1000-year reign of Jesus here on this earth. There are orthodox Jews who are wanting to rebuild a temple but it is not as a result of anything scriptural. In fact, we are aware of articles that are being made or accumulated that would be used to furnish or decorate the temple. When we take a serious look at Scripture, it is understood there is no further temple worship as a part of any future plan of the Lord. Understanding that most of Old Testament and New Testament prophecies have been fulfilled leaves little room for any future signs to be observed and only a few end-times prophecies left to be completed. I will be addressing those end-times prophecies in the closing section and chapter titled "Unfulfilled Prophecies".

There are many more things that we could discuss in Revelation but find it unnecessary to do that in light of the issues we have already written about in this book. Pastor Dan has given us great insight regarding his observations about Revelation in the two chapters titled "Let the Symbols Speak" and "You Can't Read Revelation Chronologically".

Review

To whom did John write this book?

Who is the beast in Revelation and how was he specifically identified?

What is the mark of the beast?

How and why did Nero persecute Christians?

What are some of the ways Nero was identified as a god?

What did John write to identified Rome as to where the beast lived?

Are there any Scriptures pointing to a rebuilding of the temple?

CHAPTER 9
WHEN WAS REVELATION WRITTEN

Why is it necessary to know when John wrote the book of Revelation and what is the significance that it has on end-times prophecy? This chapter will answer that and many other questions regarding this important material. Many people find the book hard to understand and in fact avoid reading it because of all of the symbolism, metaphors and mystery that seem to abound in the writings presented by John. We trust this will be a step in helping you begin to see the truths presented here and that Revelation will become more clear and understandable to you. Knowing **when** it was written is critical to **why** it was written and **who** it is written about.

Let's first look at **who** it was written to and this may help understand the significance of the symbolism and style of writing. It was a common practice of the day that the style of Hebrew writings and teachings was done using symbols and allegories. The Jewish people would have understood this style while others (Gentiles), for the most part, would have been at a loss to explain. The seven churches that John was addressing were, for the most part, Jewish and therefore the ideas and teaching in Revelation would have been easier for them to understand.

The idea of when John wrote Revelation has been a

source of controversy for the most part since the teaching of a pre-tribulation rapture of the church became so popular in the early 1800s. There are two main camps on when John wrote this, one dating around AD95 and the other in the AD60s (probably about AD67 or so). We will address both of these views in this chapter and where they came from.

Irenaeus

Those who believe that it was written around AD95 support their belief on very little questionable information. It is mainly supported by one early church father named Irenaeus and others who quoted him. There is no internal indication that John wrote the book at a date later than the destruction of Jerusalem. However, there are many internal supporting verses to indicate that it was written prior to AD70 and the destruction of Jerusalem.

Let's look at what Irenaeus said and see whether it has any credibility or not. Irenaeus said this traditional idea was passed down to him by word of mouth from his youth. He claimed Polycarp, a student of John the Revelator, related this to him in his youth. The following is what Irenaeus said. Notice that he was not really addressing when John wrote Revelation, but was addressing who the antichrist was.

"We therefore do not run the risk of pronouncing positively concerning the name of the antichrist (beast) [hidden in the number 666 in Rev.13:18], for if it were necessary to have his name distinctly announced at the present time, it would doubtless have been announced by him who saw the apocalypse; for **it is not a great while ago that it [or he] was seen**, but almost in our own generation, toward the end of Domitian's reign."[62]

The all-important part of Irenaeus' words are these: "**for it is not a great while ago that it [or he] was seen**". The Greek could intend for us to mean "he" since the Greek could be translated either "it" or "he". If Irenaeus meant the "revelation" was seen, then this calls for a late date of the book. But if he meant John was seen, then the Revelation was written earlier since Irenaeus contrasts the time of his generation from the time of the issue at hand by saying, "for it is not a great while ago that it [or he] was seen, **but almost in our own generation...**"

Irenaeus was a mere youth in Asia Minor when Polycarp would have spoken to him. He moved to Gaul (now France) before he became an adult. Should we base a very important point upon such weak and questionable evidence?

Also, Irenaeus made some other very erroneous statements regarding Jesus. **He taught that Jesus had**

---

[62] Irenaeus "Against Heresies, 5:30:3" dated AD175–AD180

a public ministry of over 15 years and that He lived to be nearly fifty. This statement is clearly in contrast to what has always been accepted and taught that Jesus lived to be about 33 and ministered for about 3½ years. This alone should make us suspicious of the credibility of Irenaeus.

With that in mind, I believe that Irenaeus may have been a good church father but a poor historian. It is, at least, questionable to use someone such as Irenaeus to support a belief in the dating of when John wrote the book of Revelation. I will cite you several examples that refute the idea that Revelation was written in AD90-95.

It seems far more reasonable to conclude that Irenaeus was speaking about John being seen, and not the revelation John saw when he wrote that "it/he" was almost in Irenaeus' generation. You see, the point of the paragraph was the refusal of John to risk naming the beast due to the Roman persecution at that time if it was (as we believe it was) speaking of Nero. He claimed he could not dare risk stating who the beast was since it would have been written in John's writing. So, to say that John lived only a short time before Irenaeus' generation, instead of the Revelation being seen just shortly before Irenaeus' generation, would make more sense in the overall point being made. If John did not write the name of the beast, and John lived just shortly before Irenaeus' generation, then how could it be possible for anyone in Irenaeus' day to be able to identify the beast? Compare that with the thought that Irenaeus spoke of the apocalypse (vision) John had. People claiming the name of the beast are the subject. Speaking of John rather than the actual revelation he saw would make more contextual sense. In fact, Irenaeus just spoke of John's person before this clause, as follows: "if it were necessary to have his name distinctly announced at the present time, it would doubtless have been announced by **him who saw the apocalypse or vision**; for it is not a great while ago that it [or he] was seen..." So now let's clarify Irenaeus' statement by reading it like this. **It is not a great while ago that he (meaning John) was seen**. This also fits with the idea from the statement that John would have still been alive during the reign of Domitian. We know from history that John left the isle of Patmos and sometime later ministered to the church at Ephesus. If John wrote Revelation in AD95, as the late date advocates propose, and then went to Ephesus to minister, he would have been quite old and probably not able to serve in a leadership role.

It is my belief that Irenaeus was referring to the idea that Nero should not be named since Irenaeus lived in a time when persecution against the church was still high. To name Nero in Revelation, rather than write "666", would incite a terrible backlash from Rome since Irenaeus' generation was not far removed from the time of John's persecution by Rome since Rome was still fighting the church heavily.

Why should Irenaeus and those in his day run the risk of announcing Nero as the beast if John, who lived shortly before, did not?

Let's look at what some other early church fathers wrote about this subject.

An ancient writing called the **Muratorian Canon**, dated at about AD170–AD210, reads, "Paul, following the order of his own predecessor John, writes to no more than seven churches by name." Those churches Paul wrote to were: Rome, Corinth, Galatia, Ephesus, Philippi, Colossi and Thessalonica. John wrote to seven churches according to Rev 1:4. This would imply that Paul wrote to seven churches after John wrote to seven churches? If Paul followed his predecessor John in this pattern of writing to seven churches, then John had to write to seven churches before Paul did! And Paul died in AD68. **This would clearly show that John wrote Revelation before Paul died.**

Several **Syriac** translations of Revelation all include this note about Revelation: "The Revelation, which was made by God to John the Evangelist, in the island of Patmos, to which he was **banished by Nero the Emperor.**" (Editor's note: Nero died in AD68)

Clement of Alexandria lived from AD150 to AD215. He wrote: "For the teaching of our Lord at His advent, beginning with Augustus and Tiberius, was completed in the middle of the times of Tiberius. And that of the apostles, embracing the ministry of Paul, end with Nero."

ANDREAS OF CAPPADOCIA

Andreas claimed Revelation was written in Nero's day.

ARETHAS around AD540 made the following strong statement regarding when Revelation was written, verifying that it was before the destruction of Jerusalem.

"For there were many, yea, a countless multitude from among the Jews, who believed in Christ: as even they testify, who said to St Paul on his arrival at Jerusalem: Thou seest, brother, how many thousands of Jews there are which believe. (Acts xxi. 20.) **And He who gave this revelation to the Evangelist, declares, that these men shall not share the destruction inflicted by the Romans. For the ruin brought by the Romans had not yet fallen upon the Jews, when this Evangelist received these prophecies**: and he did not receive them at Jerusalem, but in Ionia near Ephesus. For after the suffering of the Lord he remained only fourteen years at Jerusalem, during which time the tabernacle of the mother of the Lord, which had conceived this Divine offspring, was preserved in this temporal life, after the suffering and resurrection of her incorruptible Son. For he continued with her as with a mother committed to him by the Lord. For after her death it is reported that he no longer chose to remain in Judaea, but passed over to Ephesus, where, as we have said, **this present Apocalypse also was composed ; which is a revelation of future things, inasmuch as forty years after the ascension of the Lord this tribulation came upon the Jews**."[63]

Since there is an abundance of evidence refuting the late date belief of when John wrote the book of which I have only quoted a few, I simply must conclude that there is one simple reason that futurists choose to believe in an AD95 date. That is to simply deny John was talking about the destruction of Jerusalem. With that approach then they are free to try and apply the writings to some other future time period. In consideration of the weak foundation futurists have in Irenaeus' writing, surely we can conclude Revelation was indeed written before AD70 and was about the then-coming destruction of Jerusalem. This is the best reason we have to help understand the book of Revelation.

We have listed several more writers and church fathers who believe Revelation was written prior to AD70 in Appendix 3 at the back of this book.

---

[63] See Glossary for "Arethas"

Review

Why is the date of when Revelation was written so important?

Was Irenaeus a credible witness?

Is the early date evidence credible?

Does the book of Revelation indicate that it was written before the fall of Jerusalem?

Please read Appendix 3 and see if you get a clearer picture of the early date.

Chapter 10

LET THE SYMBOLS SPEAK

Tools for Interpreting Revelation - Part 1

I want to start this chapter with a question: Why was Revelation and other apocalyptic literature written in historical symbols?

God in His infinite wisdom wanted to reveal prophecy, which is history written in advance from God's viewpoint, in such a way as to give His people throughout the New Testament church age the comfort of knowing they were more than conquerors. To do so, He inspires the writer of Revelation and guides him to use *historical symbols*. I tell the reader this because there has been a misrepresentation of what is meant by a *literal* interpretation of Scripture by those who teach a pre-tribulation rapture. Pre-tribulation teachers use a wooden and stiff definition of *literal* as a defense and a weapon to oppose those who differ with their mistaken teaching concerning the pre-tribulation rapture, the Great Tribulation, and the Millennium. However, to interpret the Bible *literally* is to interpret it as literature, and in interpreting literature, you must determine what style or type of literature you are reading. Is it prose, poetry, proverbs, types, symbols, metaphors, apocalyptic, etc.? Ignorance of genre or type of literature results in not understanding. To interpret apocalyptic literature as prose would result in ridiculousness. You would have to say that Satan looks like a dragon rather than say that Satan, like a dragon, is dangerously aggressive and threatening to persons, or in the case of Revelation--to Christians.

Let's take a look at some of the advantages of the historical symbolism that is used in apocalyptic writing.

1. Apocalyptic Symbols Cause Flashbacks and Reviews

One of the characteristics of apocalyptic Biblical writing is the use of *historical symbols* that causes the reader to have flashbacks of past historical events that serve as symbols of present or future events that duplicate or greatly resemble the historical event. *Historical symbols*, unlike allegorical literature, are rooted in actual history and help the reader to understand the present and future by moving them from the known to the unknown. They give to the Bible a synergy and connection to salvation history.[64]   When Jesus said in Matthew 24:15 *"So when you see standing in the holy place the abomination that causes desolation, spoken of through the prophet Daniel—let the reader understand— then let those who are in Judea flee to the mountains.",* He was telling the disciples that the near future destruction of the temple would be another imitation of

---

[64] It is important for the reader of apocalyptic writing to remember that symbolic interpretation is different from allegory in that allegory has no historical roots and can be interpreted mystically. Symbolic and spiritual interpretations are rooted in actual historical events and have literal applications.

the "abomination of desolation" that Daniel foretold concerning Antiochus Epiphanes (Daniel 9:27; 11:31; 12:11). When Jesus uses Daniel's past prophecy of Antiochus Epiphanes' desecration of the temple, a past fulfilled event of Daniel's prophecy that is recorded in history, He is telling them that just as Antiochus desecrated their holy temple in the past, the temple will again be desecrated and destroyed in the immediate future. That desecration started in AD63 and culminated in AD70 by the leveling of the temple and the siege of Titus.

If it be argued that the destruction of the temple and the attack on Jerusalem is a type of what will occur right before Christ comes back at the end of the world, then pre-tribulation teachers are caught with the fact that there was no rapture or removal of the true believer from the earth before the destruction and severe tribulation or distress that came upon Jerusalem in AD70.

The dispensationalists believe that Matthew chapter 24 takes place during the seven years of tribulation after the Lord has secretly come and raptured the church out of this world. They will be protected from the events Jesus is speaking about in that chapter because they are in heaven with the Lord. The "elect", which refers to any and all believers, both Old Testament and New Testament believers, that were spared during the seven years of tribulation under Nero and the Roman Caesars (AD63-AD70), was not by a rapture or miraculous physical removal from the earth. Rather, they were saved physically while going through it as the following verses declare:

Matthew 24:21-22: (NIV)

[21]*For then there will be great distress, unequaled from the beginning of the world until now—and never to be equaled again.*[22]*"If those days had not been cut short, no one would survive, but for the sake of the elect those days will be shortened.*

Jesus uses a historical account to symbolize and represent what would happen in the near future under Titus the Great who desecrated and destroyed the Jewish temple which would never be rebuilt to serve as the symbol of Israel's spiritual status as God's elect nation. Israel's failure to obey God as a nation and their rejection of the fulfillment of Christ as the Messiah made them disqualified and to be replaced, not by a nation, but by a kingdom of people from all nations, thus fulfilling the promise made to Abraham in Genesis 1:1-4.

The main point, however, is to remember "historical symbolism" is rooted in actual history and serves to cause "flashbacks" to the known historical event, so that the unknown might be better understood.

2. Apocalyptic Historical Symbols Give Previews

What was about to happen in AD64-AD70 to Israel and the early Christian Church would serve as a preview (prototype, symbol, pictogram) of the conflicts between the world's systems of government and the government of God throughout the entire New Testament church age. Keep in mind that when Revelation was written its symbols were understood by first century Christians who needed to be encouraged in their faith.

Hank Hanegraaff clearly writes, "The beast of Revelation is not just a twenty-first-century character. He is a first-century historical character that characterizes the world's leaders throughout the church age, and the events in the Book of Revelation were meant to reveal the apocalyptic events surrounding the destruction of Jerusalem—events that were still in John's future, but are in our past. If Revelation is principally a book that describes what is about to take place in the twenty-first century, it would have been largely irrelevant to first-century Christians. "[65]

Therefore, when you read the Book of Revelation about the Beast and his actions, remember that these were actual events and people known to the first century Christians which served as examples of events that would be reoccurring over and over again throughout the New

---

[65] Hanegraaff, Hank. *The Apocalypse Code, [Thomas Nelson: Nashville] c-2007. Pgs 157-159*

Testament church age. The events recorded in Revelation were real historical events of the past that were divinely selected by the Holy Spirit to reflect the ongoing struggle the church would have which leads up to the actual visible, physical, second coming of Christ.

In a sense, God was reminding Christians that because of the fall of man, without the intervention of God to change humans' hearts, men and governments will continue to repeat the same sins of the past. Again, the only thing that natural, non-redeemed humanity learns from history is that they don't learn anything. Revelation is a reminder that our fallen world will never be a utopia by human effort and will not get better until the Lord Jesus Christ comes back to make all things new.

Review: Historical symbolism uses reviews to present previews of the conditions that all believers may have to cope with throughout the New Testament church age.

3. Apocalyptic Historical Symbols Span Generations

Symbols last longer and are more universal than words which can change from one generation to another. For example, when I was growing up I watched the Flintstones and would hear the song that said: "Have a gay ol' time" over and over again. The word "gay" then had a different meaning than the word "gay" does now. In less than fifty years the word has changed in its popular meaning. Symbols do not change in meaning that quickly.

Since the teaching of Revelation was going to

represent the struggle between the present world systems and the kingdom of God on earth, symbols would best reflect the constant struggle that the people of God would face repeatedly over and over again.

4. Apocalyptic Historical Symbols Are More Able To Arouse Intense Feelings Than Prose Or Plain Language

Anyone reading the Book of Revelation will tell you that the book's symbols, understood or not, are more emotional and solicit feelings of sadness, yet hope. While words can do this, symbols that create pictures in your mind enhance the emotional feelings desired by the author.

In America, we talk about "9/11" and if we are not careful we can lose the impact of that tragedy. However, when on the anniversary of 9/11, we see again the images of that day, we are moved again to feel the immensity of that tragedy. Historical symbols rekindle our emotions since they serve as word pictures that are graphic and sometimes extreme. Again, word pictures or symbols are much more able to stir our emotions than simple prose.

5. Historical Symbols Are Forms Of Pictures That Speak Volumes Of Words More Rapidly

Any person seeing a tennis shoe with a Nike check (trade) mark immediately thinks that it is a Nike shoe, "just do it", and visualizes athletes. One little check mark brings to mind more than one word; instead, like a picture, it brings other images and ideas that words alone could not convey that quickly. The use of images or symbols is even more necessary for those, like the early Christians, who could not read, because the symbols served as "icons" to help bring rapid awareness of truths that needed not to be forgotten. They understood symbols even if they did not completely understand the written word. Every person with a computer is grateful for "icons" or symbols that help them get to or from one application to another just by a quick look and a click.

In a world without technology, such as television, symbols make it possible to quickly visualize and move quickly from one scene to the other. For example, in Revelation chapters 1-3 you have a word picture created by symbols of the Christian church and Christ walking in the midst of the church; then in chapter 4 the spiritual camera moves from earth to heaven by using the very statement: "After this, I looked, and, behold, a door opened in heaven..." Just like "icons" on our computers, symbols help us to move quickly from earth to heaven to show us that what was happening on earth had a spiritual force or purpose behind what was happening during the time of the seven churches. This reminds us that our battles and trials are spiritual in nature and that we do not wrestle against flesh and blood, but against spiritual realities. Both what was happening on earth was happening at the same time in heaven. This is a form of Hebrew parallelism, which I will address in the next chapter.

6. Historical Symbols Can Serve As Coded Messages With Meanings Only Apparent To The Group To Which They Were Written

This was important to the church at the time Revelation was written and in this author's view, which was around AD64-AD69 because of the persecutions they were suffering and would continue to suffer throughout the New Testament church age. Many of the symbols are Hebraic and grounded in Old Testament terminology and symbols. They would only be understood by Jews, the early Jewish Christians and people who were knowledgeable of the Old Testament.

Anyone hearing or reading the description of Jesus Christ and who had any knowledge of the Old Testament would gain from the symbolic descriptions of Him. There are many descriptive meanings of who Christ was and what He did. He appears dressed as a priest because He is our high priest. He appears as walking in the midst of the seven golden candlesticks because that is what a priest did. He kept the candles lit just as Christ keeps the church, which is the light of the world, shining forth with the truth. This is a picture of the resurrected Christ who ever lives to intercede and minister to His followers. The white hair is a symbol that gives, at least, three aspects of Christ's ministry and reminds the Christians then and now that "He is the ancient of days", "He suffered for our sins". Have you ever heard your mother say, "You give me gray hair"? When you see a person with white hair you think of wisdom and Christ is our wisdom. The fact that it says His hair is white as wool makes you think of a lamb because we get wool from lambs or sheep and Christ is the Lamb of God. One word could not convey that many truths, but one symbol gives us a picture that conveys many truths, thus leaving to the reader or hearer of the text no doubt about to whom the author is referring.

7. Historical Symbols Make Use Of Exaggeration And Hyperbole For Emphases

Think of going to the county fair and having an artist draw a caricature of you. Usually, they will exaggerate or distort your nose, chin, or ears so as to make a parody of you. However, apocalyptic writing does the same exaggeration for emphases sake but not for humor. When you see an enormous red dragon with seven heads and seven horns or locusts with human faces and fire coming out of their tails, they do not resemble anything you want to meet in real life. A dragon which is a fantasy symbol represents Satan, evil, danger and solicits fear, but a real life symbol like a lamb represents Jesus Christ, the "Lamb of God who takes away the sins of the world". The exaggerated, historical symbol can intensify the image in order to cause the reader to sense the nature of the image much like hyperbole does in writing. If I say it is "raining cats and dogs", you don't look for "cats and dogs" falling from the sky because you know I am saying that it is raining extremely hard.

8. Apocalyptic Writing Such as Revelation Makes Great Use of Numbers That Serve as Symbols

In common with most people in the ancient world, the Israelites attached symbolic significance to numbers. So when a biblical writer mentions a number in apocalyptic writings, they most generally are symbolic and not literal.

One symbolizes uniqueness or undivided wholeness or both. "Hear, O Israel; YHWH is our God, YHWH is one" (Deuteronomy 6:4), means not only that the God of Israel is unique, but also that there is no contradiction within Him. The oneness of God, therefore, calls for the trust and love of His people (Deut. 6:5). As God is one, so some New Testament writers insist Christ is one with the Father (John 10:30; 17:21); therefore His people must be one (John 17:21; Ephesians 4:4-6).

Two, the smallest number larger than one, was the minimum number of witnesses required to establish the truth (Deuteronomy 19:15; John 8:17-18; Revelation 11:3-4).

Three is widely regarded as a divine number. Just look at the Trinity. The temple was divided into three parts (I Kings 6). Three days was the proper time for a work of God, which meant, by the ancient reckoning of time, that it was completed on the third day (Exodus 19:11; Mark 8:31; I Corinthians 15:4). Time is divided into three parts: the past, present, and future, and God is He who is, who was, and is to come (Revelation 1:8).

Three and a half years is a strictly limited period, half the full seven of God's plan. It was regarded as significant that there were three and a half years between the desecration of the Temple and its rededication (Daniel 7:25; Revelation 11:2-3).[66]

Four is the number of the created world. There are four corners of the earth, four wind directions, four seasons, and four kinds of living creatures: human, domestic animals, wild animals, and creatures of the sea and sky (Genesis 1:20-27; Ezekiel 1:10; Revelation 4:6-7). There were four horsemen of Revelation who had four different purposes, and we have four Gospels signifying the universality of the Gospel.

Five is the number of fingers on one hand and could stand for a handful, or a few.

Six is a number that can represent incompleteness. The six days of creation were not complete until the seventh day of rest had come. In the book of Revelation six seals, trumpets, etc. represent the course of the world before the final seventh act brings about the eternal Sabbath or rest for His people. The number "666" represents man and the incomplete effort of the

---

[66] It should be noted that unlike other destructions of the temple in the Old Testament there followed a three-day rededication. The destruction of the temple, which Matthew 24 deals with, is final and never to be rebuilt as a true spiritual temple because Christ fulfilled the temple images that pointed to the true heavenly temple of God.

governments of the world to accomplish only what God "777" can accomplish and make perfect.

Seven, the sum of three plus four, of heaven and earth, signifies completeness and perfection. There are seven chief heavenly bodies (sun, moon, and five planets known to ancients), seven days of the week, seven archangels, seven sabbatical years, the seven spirits of Revelation representing the seven-fold perfection of the Holy Spirit. Seven churches represent the universal church throughout the church age (Revelation 1:20). It is necessary to forgive, not just seven times, but seventy times seven times (Matthew 18:21-22). We will see in the next chapter that the Book of Revelation takes you through the entire New Testament church age seven (7) times from different views.

Eight was later used for God's new creation, the day of the Resurrection being regarded as the eighth day rather than the first, or seventh day Sabbath.

Ten is simply a round number, the number of the fingers on both hands. "And God said" ten times in creation of the world (Genesis 1:1-2:4) and He gave us Ten Commandments by which to govern the world. However, ten, a thousand, ten thousand, are used simply to signify small or large numbers as a form of rounding off.

Twelve, like seven, is a number of completeness and perfection. This number must not be taken literally.

Israel always comprised more than twelve tribes (Genesis 49; Joshua 13-19; Revelation 7:7-8). But the number twelve meant "all of Israel" or "all of God's people". The twenty-four elders (12+12) in Revelation 4:4 represents all of God's people, which includes all of spiritual Israel (Revelation 7) and all the Gentiles from every nation that could not be numbered by humans.

Thirty was the age at which one was believed to reach full maturity (Gen. 41-46; Numbers 4:3-2; Luke 3:23).

Forty years was the length of one generation (Exodus 16:35; Numbers 14:33).

Jesus' Coming In The Clouds
(Visible Or Symbolic)

There are some apocalyptic symbols that need to be addressed due to the misunderstanding and interpretation of what those symbols mean.

The first thing that needs to be addressed is whether Jesus is literally coming in the clouds or is this apocalyptic language. Is this a visible coming or a symbolic one? Jesus coming in clouds or with the clouds has been so twisted by dispensationalists, because of their belief that this is a literal/physical coming, that it has become utter confusion to try and follow their teaching.

In fact, in some cases, many of them do not agree with each other regarding the understanding. Since we are looking at symbols that are included in Revelation, let's begin by looking at Revelation 1:7. The symbol of clouds is mentioned several times in Scripture and refers to God's judgment.

Revelation 1:7 (NIV)

[7]"Look, he is coming with the clouds," and "every eye will see him, even those who pierced him"; and all peoples on earth "will mourn because of him." So shall it be! Amen.

There is a passage in Daniel that is cross-referenced to this verse. So for clarity and understanding, let's look at it also.

Daniel 7:9-13 (NIV)

[9]"As I looked, "thrones were set in place, and the Ancient of Days took his seat. His clothing was as white as snow; the hair of his head was white like wool. His throne was flaming with fire, and its wheels were all ablaze. [10]A river of fire was flowing, coming out from before him. Thousands upon thousands attended him; ten thousand times ten thousand stood before him. The court was seated, and the books were opened. [11]"Then I continued to watch because of the boastful words the horn was speaking. I kept looking until the beast was slain and its

body destroyed and thrown into the blazing fire. [12](The other beasts had been stripped of their authority, but were allowed to live for a period of time.) [13]"In my vision at night I looked, and there before me was one like a son of man coming with the clouds of heaven. He approached the Ancient of Days and was led into his presence.

The title "Ancient of Days" first appears in Daniel 7:9, where Daniel is describing his vision of heaven. There is an ancient person who sits on a flaming throne with wheels of fire, His hair and clothing white as snow. The flaming throne is symbolic of judgment, while the white hair and title "Ancient" indicate that God existed before time began.

There can be no doubt that the reference in Daniel 7 is pointing to God as Judge. A similar description occurs in Revelation 1:14-15, wherein Christ is described as having snow-white hair and blazing eyes. In Revelation, God the Son is depicted with the same power of judgment over His church as the Ancient of Days is described as having in judging Israel. In fact, His sharp gaze judges all seven of the churches in Revelation 1–3.

The title "Ancient of Days" is found only three times in Scripture, and all three are in prophetic passages written in Daniel 7:9,13, and 22. Verse 22 refers specifically to Jesus who judges Israel. In Daniel 7:13, the term "Ancient of Days" refers to God the Father, and we see Him on His throne as Jesus, the "Son of Man", approaches the throne on clouds. God is a triune God, meaning three Persons in One, and at different times "Ancient of Days" refers to Jesus Christ, and at other times to God the Father. But in the prophetic sense, it clearly refers to Jesus, the Ancient of Days, returning to pronounce judgment on the seven churches. It also refers to Matthew 24:30 which is clearly a symbolic coming of Jesus regarding the destruction of Jerusalem.

Matthew 24:30 (NIV)

30Then will appear the sign of the Son of Man in heaven. And then all the peoples of the earth will mourn when they see the Son of Man coming on the clouds of heaven, with power and great glory.

This statement by Jesus regarding the "Son of Man" coming on the clouds is a direct reference pointing to the destruction of Jerusalem in AD70. Our chapter in section one titled "The Great Tribulation" gives a more detailed explanation of this along with many other Scriptures regarding the destruction of Jerusalem.

Let's look at another reference by Jesus regarding His "coming on the clouds".

Matthew 26:63-65 (NIV)

⁶³But Jesus remained silent. The high priest said to him, "I charge you under oath by the living God: Tell us if you are the Messiah, the Son of God." ⁶⁴"You have said so," Jesus replied. "But I say to all of you: From now on you will see the Son of Man sitting at the right hand of the Mighty One and coming on the clouds of heaven." ⁶⁵Then the high priest tore his clothes and said, "He has spoken blasphemy! Why do we need any more witnesses? Look, now you have heard the blasphemy."

There are those who try to place this event, mentioned by Jesus in verse 64, at the end of the world when Jesus returns at His second coming. When Jesus made this statement to the high priest, He knew that the high priest would understand the symbolism of the Lord coming in judgment. The high priest would not literally see Jesus in heaven on a throne, but knew only God could come in judgment. The high priest would remember Daniel's writing in chapter 7 regarding the "Son of Man" coming with clouds in judgment. Jesus did not use speech that was unfamiliar to the high priest. The high priest knew exactly what Jesus was insinuating and that is why he accused Jesus of blasphemy. He understood that Jesus was claiming to be the God of the Old Testament. Jesus not only informed the high priest that He was God, but also that Jerusalem would be judged just as she was judged in Old Testament times. Again, Jesus was referring to the coming destruction of Jerusalem in AD70.

Jesus said to His disciples in Matthew 16:28 that there would be some standing there who would not taste of death before they saw His coming.

Matthew 16:28 (NIV)

28Truly I tell you, some who are standing here will not taste death before they see the Son of Man coming in his kingdom.

There are several references to clouds and the judgment of God in Scripture. Here are just a few. You may wish to study this more in depth by reading Jeremiah 4:13-14, Nahum 1:3, Zephaniah 1:15-17 as well as many others.

Sun, Moon And Stars

Several verses have been misinterpreted by futurists that are used in Scripture of the sun, moon, and stars. I have spent a considerable amount of time and looked at literally dozens of opinions regarding this subject. It appears that many, if not most of the futurists, look at these symbols as something to do with the last day associated with the Lord's final and visible return. Their interpretation seems to indicate a relationship with the destruction of the universe which Peter describes in II Peter 3:10 and does appear to be literal.

II Peter 3:10 (NIV)

¹⁰But the day of the Lord will come like a thief. The heavens will disappear with a roar; the elements will be destroyed by fire, and the earth and everything done in it will be laid bare.

This symbolic picture of an apocalyptic writing has been so misinterpreted that I found it necessary to address it. The better and clearer approach to this teaching in God's Word is not a literal view, but a symbolic view. The above passage written by Peter is referring to the final end when Jesus does return to reap the harvest spoken about in Matthew chapter 13. The following Scriptures are but a few recorded in the Bible referring to the sun being darkened, the moon not giving its light and the stars falling from the sky. Let's see if this agrees with the popular belief of being associated with the final day when the Lord returns for His people and the ultimate destruction of the universe. Or is there another understanding which better fits the truth found in these verses.

Matthew 24:29-33 (NIV)

²⁹Immediately after the distress of those days "'the sun will be darkened, and the moon will not give its light; the stars will fall from the sky, and the heavenly bodies will be shaken.' ³⁰Then will appear the sign of the Son of Man in heaven. And then all the peoples of the earth will mourn when they see the Son of Man coming on the clouds of heaven, with power and great glory. *31*And he will send his angels with a loud trumpet call, and they will gather his elect from the four winds, from one end of the heavens to the other. *32*Now learn this lesson from the fig tree: As soon as its twigs get tender and its leaves come out, you know that summer is near. *33*Even so, when you see all these things, you know that it is near, right at the door.

Ezekiel 32:7 (NIV)

*7*When I snuff you out, I will cover the heavens and darken their stars; I will cover the sun with a cloud, and the moon will not give its light.

Joel 2:10 (NIV)

*10*Before them the earth shakes, the heavens tremble, the sun and moon are darkened, and the stars no longer shine.

Joel 3:15 (NIV)

*15*The sun and moon will be darkened, and the stars no longer shine.

Revelation 6:12-13 (NIV)

*12*I watched as he opened the sixth seal. There was a great earthquake. The sun turned black like sackcloth made of goat hair, the whole moon turned blood red, *13* and the stars in the sky fell to earth, as figs drop from a fig tree when shaken by a strong wind.

In Matthew 24:29 when Jesus was teaching about the "sun will be darkened, and the moon will not give its light; the stars will fall from the sky, and the heavenly bodies will be shaken", He was quoting Isaiah 13:9-10.

Isaiah 13:9-10 (NIV)

⁹See, the day of the LORD is coming—a cruel day, with wrath and fierce anger—to make the land desolate and destroy the sinners within it. ¹⁰The stars of heaven and their constellations will not show their light. The rising sun will be darkened and the moon will not give its light.

"Surely no one supposes that the stars went into supernova when Isaiah pronounced judgment on Babylon in 539BC. Instead, as Isaiah used the sun, moon, and stars as metaphors against Babylon, our Lord used them as judgment images against Jerusalem. Indeed, only when we interpret Scripture in light of Scripture rather than Scripture in light of a daily newspaper do we perceive its perspicuous [or true] meaning."[67] Brackets added by the author.

There are several other Scriptures that parallel these passages. So what do these verses mean or how do we understand them? It's important to see these are clearly symbolic prophecies of the wrath and anger of God and cannot possibly be viewed as literal. As with the coming in clouds by Jesus, this too is a clear indication of

[67] The Apocalypse Code, Hank Hanegraaff, Thomas Nelson publishing 2007 page 233

His judgment. As an example, when we look at Rev. 6:17 which describes what is happening with the opening of the sixth seal, we can see it plainly tells us of God's wrath.

Revelation 6:17 (NIV)

17For the great day of His wrath has come, and who can withstand it?

For anyone to think this is a literal event and not apocalyptic is simply ignoring the obvious. The clear reading of these and other supporting Scriptures will give us the comprehension to realize that God's anger will seem to be as if these events are literally happening.

When we look at the accompanying verses that surround each of these passages, we can begin to get an idea of the proper view. Let's look specifically at Matthew 24:29-33; the events appear as follows. Verse 29 says immediately after the distress of those days, the sun shall be darkened, the moon will not give her light and the stars will fall from heaven. Then in verse 30, the sign of the "Son of Man" will appear in heaven and then all the tribes of earth will mourn. This is not the Gentiles, but all of the tribes will mourn. The Jews are identified many times in Scripture as tribes. This would be clearly understood by those in their day that Jesus was teaching about the judgment of the Jews. The next thing that will happen is they will see the "Son of Man" coming in the clouds of heaven with power and great glory. We have just dealt with this, showing that coming in clouds is a judgmental coming and not a literal physical visible event. In the next three verses (verses 31-33) we see a gathering of His elect, the parable of the fig tree, and Jesus telling the disciples that the time is near. Now then, if the time is near, just how soon is near? Verse 34 tells us that very plainly, so let's look at it.

Matthew 24:34 (NIV)

³⁴Truly I tell you, this generation will certainly not pass away until all these things have happened.

What generation is Jesus talking about? It certainly cannot be 2000 years later as the dispensationalists would have you believe. Remember, we understand Jesus has been telling the disciples about the destruction of Jerusalem and the temple which happened in AD67-AD70. Then if this generation will not pass away before "all these things have happened", He was telling them it would occur in their day, not 2000 years later.

In Genesis 37:9 & 10, Jacob clearly understood that he was symbolically being represented as the sun, his wife was the moon, and his children were the stars.

Genesis 37:9-10 (NIV)

⁹Then he had another dream, and he told it to his brothers. "Listen," he said, "I had another dream, and this time the sun and moon and eleven stars were bowing down to me." ¹⁰When he told his father as well as his brothers, his father rebuked him and said, "What is this dream you had? Will your mother and I and your brothers actually come and bow down to the ground before you?"

This was the beginning of the nation of Israel. Remember, God changed Jacob's name to Israel. In Revelation chapter 12, these symbols are used to identify the nation of Israel and refers to them throughout the chapter. In verse 1, Israel is described as a woman clothed with the sun and moon and wearing a crown of stars. This parallels the symbols to Joseph's dream in Genesis 37. In the next verse, Israel is the woman about to give birth.

Verse 5 identifies her child as the Messiah, Jesus Christ, the One born to rule all nations and He was caught up to God and His throne.

It is not until verse 17 that the remnant comes directly into the picture, identified as "the rest of her offspring, who keep the commandments of God and have the testimony of Jesus Christ", the Messiah born to the woman in verse 5. Israel, the nation, does not keep the commandments of God, nor does it have the testimony of Jesus Christ. Even as the Messiah was born of the woman and definitely kept the commandments of God, so also does the remnant of her offspring.

The sun and moon (Jacob and his wives) have stopped giving light. The tribes of Jacob (the stars) have fallen and the Jewish nation is shaken and in distress.

With Jerusalem now totally destroyed in AD70 and the majority of the Jews in the land having been killed, those who were left alive have been scattered.

Amos 9:8 (NIV)

8"Surely the eyes of the Sovereign Lord *are on the sinful kingdom. I will destroy it from the face of the earth. Yet I will not totally destroy the descendants of Jacob,"* *declares the* Lord*.*

The remnants of the 12 tribes have finally been totally scattered. Some of them were scattered in 722BC when the Assyrians came in and conquered them and then later in 597BC during the Babylonian captivity. Some of the tribes of Judah, Benjamin and Levi returned later to rebuild Jerusalem, which was totally destroyed in AD70, but they were never again to shine like the stars they once were. Most of them today do not even know what tribe they are from. They only know that they are descendants of Israel. God's judgment was devastating with the destruction of Jerusalem and the temple. Their covenant with God was totally obliterated due to their disobedience. Only the remnant which kept God's commandments have the testimony of Jesus Christ (Revelation 12:17).

No Return Rights To The Land

"There is no evidence that the apostles believed that the Jewish people still had a divine right to the land, or that the Jewish possession of the land would be important, let alone that Jerusalem would remain a central aspect of God's purposes for the world. On the contrary, in the Christological[68] logic of Paul, Jerusalem, and the land, had now been superseded. They have been made irrelevant in God's redemptive purposes."[69]

In researching the Zionist/Palestinian war of 1947 to 1949 I cannot find any conclusive evidence that the Jews who fought during that time were or are identified by any special tribe. They were just simply called Zionists. Some, mostly dispensationalists, see this invasion and war as God returning His blessing on Jews and their land. I don't see that at all. There is no Biblical inference to the Jews having the right to return to the land.

"The fall of Jerusalem is to be an act of Divine judgment, compared in a shocking way to the judgment on Babylon described by Isaiah. What seems to be most significant, therefore, is that whereas the Old Testament prophets predicted judgment, exile and a return to the land, Jesus predicts destruction and exile, but says nothing about a return to the land. Instead of predicting

---

[68] This is the field of study within Christian theology which is primarily concerned with the nature and person of Jesus as recorded in the canonical Gospels and the epistles of the New Testament.
[69] Stephen Sizer, Christian Zionism, Page170

the restoration of Israel, He speaks about a kingdom of God coming through the Son of Man".[70]

When the sun, moon and stars ceased to shine after Jerusalem was destroyed, it was and is over as far as God placing His blessing on the nation of Israel. They became apostate and not only refused Jesus as their Messiah, they had Him crucified. When they said to Pilate "let His blood be on us and our children", God took them at their word.

If we can get a grasp on this apocalyptic teaching about the sun, moon and stars as a judgment of God on Israel, and not a literal end time event when Jesus does come visibly, we can then realize that when Jesus returns, the preceding list of prophetic Scriptures will have already taken place. The sun being darkened, the moon turning to blood and the stars falling is a clear indication that the nation of Israel has been judged by God and He has taken His blessing from them.[71] It is the end of Israel as God's chosen people to carry the Gospel to the world. Israel failed to follow God's commands and carry the message of salvation to a lost and dying world. The responsibility for spreading the message of the Gospel was then placed upon the Gentiles.

---

[70] Colin Chapman, Whose Holy City?, page 42
[71] Our chapter in this book on the Great Tribulation will bring a much clearer understanding regarding the judgment of Israel.

A Change Of Understanding

Initially believing that the Jews were to occupy Palestine again as the "promised land", I was absolutely stunned to discover there is nothing recorded in Scripture that supports a return again of the Jewish people to that land. I know this will come as a shock to many of you as it did to me. The most prevalent view in recent years has been that the Jews have a right to the land and therefore God will bless them as they endeavor to re-establish the "promised land".

There are some Scriptures which can be misconstrued and twisted to make it appear that the "promised land" still belongs to the Jew, however, after careful study, when the "the sun was darkened, and the moon did not give its light; the stars fell from the sky, and the heavenly bodies were shaken", God pronounced His final judgment against Israel. Jerusalem was destroyed, the temple was gone and God's covenant relationship with Israel was forever broken. My hope is that this will allow you to more clearly understand what the difference is between symbolic and literal teachings in the Word of God.

When His final and physical/visible coming happens we will go to be with the Lord and dwell with Him forever in heaven where He has gone to prepare a place for us according to John chapter 14. It is then that the prophecy listed in II Peter 3:10 will be fulfilled. Also that is when there will be a new heaven and new earth.

This will be a new creation of the universe. Sin and its devastation will be erased because the first heaven and earth have passed away. Both the new heaven and the new earth will be a glorious and peaceful place the way God intended it to be. Here is what John saw in his vision for those of us who are faithful and obedient to God's holy calling.

Revelation 21:1-7 (NIV)

¹Then I saw "a new heaven and a new earth," for the first heaven and the first earth had passed away, and there was no longer any sea. ²I saw the Holy City, the New Jerusalem, coming down out of heaven from God, prepared as a bride beautifully dressed for her husband. ³And I heard a loud voice from the throne saying, "Look! God's dwelling place is now among the people, and he will dwell with them. They will be his people, and God himself will be with them and be their God. ⁴'He will wipe every tear from their eyes. There will be no more death' or mourning or crying or pain, for the old order of things has passed away." ⁵He who was seated on the throne said, "I am making everything new!" Then he said, "Write this down, for these words are trustworthy and true." ⁶He said to me: "It is done. I am the Alpha and the Omega, the Beginning and the End. To the thirsty I will give water without cost from the spring of the water of life. ⁷Those who are victorious will inherit all this, and I will be their God and they will be my children.

182

Conclusion

Much more could be said about why Revelation is written in historical symbols, but remember, the symbols would speak to the first century Christians as well as to Christians throughout the entire New Testament church age. To look for hidden references to credit cards, B-52 bombers, helicopters and dams that were built thousands of years later at the Tigress and Euphrates River is to superimpose on the text an interpretation that would mean nothing to the early believers and would only serve to entertain the present generation. We should not superimpose current events of the day on the Scriptures, but understand them in light of the audience they were written to. We need to understand that the early church would have realized the truth contained in the symbols and they would carry a deeper understanding of the message being conveyed.

Dispensational teachers like Tim LaHaye build "straw men" so-to-speak by falsely accusing those who don't agree with his narrow definition of "literal interpretation" as being people who "allegorize[72] or spiritualize" Scripture, rather than taking the Scriptures at face value, as the following reveals:

"One thing most of the detractors of our books have in common is a tendency to allegorize   or   spiritualize

---

[72] We do not allegorize Scripture as LeHaye states. We do believe the writers used symbols for understanding.

prophecy. Some take the rest of Scripture *literally* but insist that prophecy is somehow different. According to them, we need to be looking for some deeper, "secret meaning" other than the *literal* message conveyed by the words on the page. Once you begin heading down that road, however, everything is up for grabs. You can invent any kind of "interpretation" you want."[73]

LaHaye takes advantage of people's ignorance of the differences between literal, allegory, and spiritualizing. Allegory is not rooted in history and fact; spiritualizing is not ignoring literary genres, and to really understand the literal meaning of any literature, you must determine if the author is writing in prose, poetry, parables, or symbols, etc. To interpret apocalyptic literature as prose is to make the same error that the Jews did in understanding Christ. When our Lord said in **John 2:19: "Destroy this temple, and I will raise it again in three days.",** the Jews interpreted Jesus in literal prose way. They understood the plain-sense or commonsense meaning of Jesus' words and thought He was directly referring to the destruction of the temple when Jesus was referring to His body and the resurrection. *John 2:21: "The temple he had spoken of was his body."*

If you follow Tim LaHaye's limited and restricted definition of literal interpretation you will fail to observe

[73] Introduction to Mark Hitchcock and Thomas Ice. *The Truth Behind Left Behind: A Biblical View of the End Times* (Sisters, OR: Multnomah, 2004), pg. 13

184

what type of literature the author was using. You cannot interpret apocalyptic literature, such as Revelation, as you would prose.

LaHaye contradicts his own misunderstood and over-simplified definition of literal when he says that the word in Matthew 24 for "this generation" does not mean this generation living at the time of Christ, but refers to people in the 21st century. He also says that when Revelation says "soon" or "near" it means 2000 years later. Literal to LaHaye seems to be a form of vacillating literalism that only dispensationalists can determine, and that was previously unrecognized by all biblical scholars until the 1850s. Even though LaHaye claims to be a literalist, he will spiritualize words like "soon" and "near" as well as "this generation" when it is needed to fit his theme of dispensationalism. Soon, near, and this generation are not symbols and should be taken literally. We know that his confusing approach and interpretation of prophecy has caused many errors to be perpetrated upon the unsuspecting believer. One of the reasons we are writing this book is to point out these false teachings with the hope that the reader will dig deeper into the Word of God and see the truths presented there.

We want to get the literal meaning from the symbolic language of Revelation and that requires we understand what the symbols meant to those whom John was writing between AD63 & AD70. Remember that John uses a lot of Old Testament symbolism in the writing of

Revelation. Hopefully, this will help you understand the next chapter written by Pastor Dan concerning progressive parallelism. It is titled **"You Can't Read Revelation Chronologically"**.

CHAPTER 11

YOU CAN'T READ REVELATION CHRONOLOGICALLY

Tools for Interpreting Revelation - Part 2

The author of the Book of Revelation not only uses historical symbols in order to change scenes quickly, but he uses a form of Hebrew poetry called Progressive Parallelism to take you through the New Testament church age seven times. We refer to "Hebrew Progressive Parallelism" because the parallelism is moving you progressively to a climactic event in each section—that event being the second coming of Christ. The reason the author does this seven times and not six or some other number of times is because the number seven in Jewish literature represented "perfection or completion". God completed the work of creation by His resting on the seventh day, which represents that our final rest as the church will occur when Jesus comes again.

Hebrew Progressive Parallelism is unique to the Jews and would give great meaning to the early church that was made up predominantly of Jewish Christians and who would see the Caesars of Rome as a type of conflict the church would suffer throughout the entire church age.

Hendriksen, along with other scholars, beautifully

divides the seven sections of the Book of Revelation in which each section takes you through the entire New Testament church age. As we look at each section, the transitions from one section to another are delineated by an early reference to the life of Christ at the beginning of a new section and ends the section with a reference to the second coming. We will also see how the author focuses upon a little different event than the preceding section did, or it expands or reinforces our understanding further of the New Testament church age in which the church is engaged. The church is the primary reason for the Book of Revelation as it is the main agenda for the second coming.

Hebrew Parallelism At Work

Seven Parallel Sections

1. Christ In The Midst Of The Lampstands (Church) Revelation 1, 2 & 3 Focus: "What Happens In the Church?"

In this first parallel section, it is no surprise that the author begins with the true church, the true followers of Christ who are called out from this world to live and reflect Christ. The church, which is made up of all Old Testament believers and all New Testament believers until the second coming, is the *main reason for Christ's return.* Revelation chapters 1-3 is a picture of the church, not just one period of history as dispensationalists teach, but they represent conditions that will be constantly repeated throughout the church age. It starts with Christ's first coming to save His people spiritually (1:5) and ends with Christ's second coming to judge all the nations (1:7). The purpose of this section is to reassure them of the resurrected Christ who rules from heaven and who is also present in the midst of the church and who is helping them to fulfill their mission by keeping His promise to them.

2. The Vision Of The Heaven And The Seals
   ### Revelation 4:1-7:17
   ### Focus: "What Happens In Heaven"

This second parallel section moves quickly to heaven so as to show that what is happening in heaven during the entire church age is not ignored by heaven, but instead is being controlled from heaven and is opening doors all over the world for the Gospel to be preached. It also reminds the church that what is occurring on earth is primarily a spiritual war (Ephesians 6:10-18). It starts with a reference to Christ being slain and now ruling from heaven (5:5,6) and ends with judgment day upon the wicked (6:6-17) and God wiping away all the tears of those who have suffered (7:16, 17). Please note there is no promise of physical escape from the terrible trouble upon the earth.

3. **The Seven Trumpets**
   Revelation 8:1-11:19
   Focus: "What Happens To the World?"

   This third parallel section begins with the seven trumpets that affect the world throughout the church age and ends with the final judgment (Revelation 11:15-18). In these chapters God reveals to the church the effects of prayer. When persecuted, the church prays and sacrifices for the mission of preaching the Gospel and God answers by pouring out judgments upon the wicked, but this is not God's final and full wrath that is left to occur at the second coming. These judgments upon the earth are designed to convert the sinners, not destroy them. However, in the end, even these judgments, like Egypt under Pharaoh in the Old Testament, only caused the sinners to become more and more hardened against God and the Christians.

   The two witnesses[74] mentioned in chapter 11:3 are the church giving out the Gospel message through their persecutions and during the calamities that come upon the wicked. These calamities affect the wicked physically and spiritually. The true church is cleansed, prayerfully powerful, and through suffering shows the world that true Christians are not fair-weather followers of Christ.

---

[74] See Glossary for more on "Two Witnesses"

4. The Persecuting Dragon And His Allies
Revelation 12:1-14:20
Focus: "What the Dragon Does to Christ and the Church

The fourth parallel section begins with a very clear reference to the birth of Christ (12:5) and continues to show how Satan attempts to devour Christ until Christ is taken up to heaven. Then Satan attacks the woman or mother church (12:13). Satan employs the beast, the great harlot, Babylon (14:8). It closes with the second coming of Christ (14:14-16). The woman is the church, the child is Christ, and the dragon is Satan and his allies. There is constant tension between the church and Satan as prophesied in the Old Testament, but Satan cannot stop the onward advance of the church.

5. The Seven Bowls
Revelation 15:1-16:21
Focus: "What the Lord Does to Those Who Worship the Dragon"

The fifth parallel section points out that throughout the church age, God's wrath is being poured out upon the wicked and that wrath continues in intensity until the second coming when He will purge the earth (16:20). Those who do not know Christ are already experiencing in some way the wrath of God in this present age. Sometimes we are punished by our sins, not just for our sins.

6. The Fall Of Babylon
Revelation 17:1-19:21
Focus: "What Happens to the Great Kingdoms of the World?"

The sixth parallel section points to Babylon's fall and is announced as though it already happened. That is because Babylon's final demise is as certain as if it had happened because God declares it and knows the future as though it were the past. Babylon represents all the great governments of the world who try to establish themselves without God and whose values oppose those of believers. God's people are called to leave Babylon and her ways. The vision ends with the coming of Christ (Revelation 19:11).

7. The Great Consummation
Revelation 20:1-22:21
Focus: "What Happens to the Devil during the Church Age?"

It is in this seventh section that you find the only mention of the "millennial" or thousand year reign of Christ. This whole issue of "the thousand years" was addressed in section one in the chapter titled "The Thousand Years". It is imperative that we see Revelation 20 does not follow Revelation 19:19 which is the day of final judgment, but begins a new vision starting with the beginning of the church age and tracing it through the entire church age to the final consummation or second coming.

If you will keep the idea in mind of Hebrew parallelism and symbolism and use them as you read Revelation, they will greatly enhance your understanding of the Revelation. Again, to read the book as though it was written in chronological order rather than Hebrew Parallelism is to actually miss the meaning of the Book of Revelation and to misunderstand what the "thousand years" or the millennium refers to. (See chapter titled "The Thousand Years".)

Review

1. Why would the author use Hebrew Parallelism in writing apocalyptic Revelation?
2. Why would the writer use symbols presented here and what sense of emotion would those symbols give to the first century Christians?
3. What happens when you try to read the Book of Revelation chronologically rather than through the lenses of Hebrew Parallelism?

CHAPTER 12

THE BATTLE OF ARMAGEDDON

The chapter dealing with the "Great Tribulation" has given us a good look at what devastation the Jews went through during the first century from AD67 to AD70. We will look at one of the most popular subjects when talking about prophecy and that is "The Battle of Armageddon".[75]

Revelation 16:16-19 (NIV)

[16]Then they gathered the kings together to the place that in Hebrew is called Armageddon. [17]The seventh angel poured out his bowl into the air, and out of the temple came a loud voice from the throne, saying, "It is done!" [18]Then there came flashes of lightning, rumblings, peals of thunder and a severe earthquake. No earthquake like it has ever occurred since mankind has been on earth, so tremendous was the quake. [19]The great city split into three parts, and the cities of the nations collapsed. God remembered Babylon the Great and gave her the cup filled with the wine of the fury of his wrath.

---

[75] See Glossary for "Armageddon"

The word "Armageddon" is only mentioned once in the entire Bible. You would think because of the popularity of this topic there would be many verses addressing this issue, but it is only found in the above passage of Scripture. Whole doctrines have been built on the premise that this is found throughout the prophecies of both the Old and New Testaments. This subject is entirely absent from the Old Testament. It is interesting that many Christians, as well as many non-Christians, believe that this is some kind of future cataclysmic battle which will involve the whole world and may well be considered the end of time as we know it. When we look closely at this Scripture, we will see this is not a valid interpretation of what the futurists are teaching and certainly falls within the realm of a vivid imagination.

Let's look at what was revealed to John in this writing to the early church. We have given you much information about the timing of the destruction of Jerusalem in previous chapters and how most of the book of Revelation pointed to the judgment of the Jews by God. If what we have written is valid, then this Scripture must also be referring to that same time.

"Battles were fought at Megiddo: Barak and Deborah overthrew the armies of the Canaanite king, Jabin, and the Midianites (Judges 5:19), and King Josiah was killed by Pharaoh Neco (2 Kings 23:29). Modern advocates of the Armageddon doctrine have combined these and other Megiddo battles into one great future

"Great Tribulation" conflict where the antichrist will bring all nations of the world into a final war against Israel."[76]

As we have said before, we must interpret Scripture in light of Scripture. In our chapter on understanding Revelation, it is important to realize that Revelation is interpreted in light of the rest of prophecy. We don't "bend" all other Scriptures to fit what we think Revelation is saying.

Megiddo in the Old Testament is a reference to many battles between rival kings and kingdoms. With this being the case, we must realize that in this passage Revelation is referring to another battle between kingdoms. "Israel remembered Megiddo as a place where God vented His divine wrath against rebellion, whether exhibited by Israel or a foreign power. God brought the nations of the world against first century Jerusalem as He had promised (Matt.22:7; 24:14). Rome, as an "empire of nations" (Syria, Asia Minor, Palestine, Gaul, Egypt, Britain, and others) representing all the nations of the world (see Luke 21), came up against Jerusalem and destroyed her."[77] There were some who actually tried to fight "the beast" of Rome but lost their life. King Josiah is a prime example of this.

---

[76] Last Days Madness, Gary DeMar, American Vision, Powder Springs GA. Page 317
[77] ibid page 318

The battle does not take place in the valley of Megiddo but in the city. Which city? Revelation 11:8 tells exactly where.

Revelation 11:8 (NIV)

[8]Their bodies will lie in the public square of the great city—which is figuratively called Sodom and Egypt—where also their Lord was crucified.

Jerusalem had many nicknames such as being called Sodom, Egypt, and Babylon. These nicknames for Jerusalem reflect the characteristics of these wicked cities. Jerusalem was also called the "great city" and our Lord was crucified there. Remember, God is bringing judgment on the Jews for what they did to Jesus. What they asked for in Matthew chapter 27:25, they received.

Matthew 27:25 (NIV)

[25]All the people answered, "His blood is on us and on our children!"

So we can see from this Scripture the location of the battle is not in the valley of Megiddo but is in Jerusalem. A study will show that the plain of Megiddo was in view from Jerusalem. This judgment of God on Jerusalem recorded in this Apocalypse[78] is another support for Revelation being written prior to AD70.

---

[78] See Glossary for "Apocalypse"

"Josephus tells us that when Titus left Egypt with orders from his father [Vespasian] to subdue the Jews, he returned to Caesarea, having taken a resolution to gather all his other forces together at that place. Bear in mind that Caesarea was within sight of Mt. Carmel, the mountain of Megiddo, and those armed forces coming from the northern regions must pass through Megiddo before reaching the appointed place of gathering. Titus stayed in the regions around Caesarea until most of the forces from the north arrived, and then moved on to Jerusalem for the "battle of the great day of God Almighty."[79]

It doesn't matter if we see this battle as symbolic or another literal war with Israel, it's over. Knowing what Jesus said to His disciples in Matthew 24 was going to happen within their lifetime, and that the book of Revelation depicts mostly first century events, we must conclude that the "Battle of Armageddon" was correctly prophesied by Jesus and fulfilled before the end of AD70.

John wrote many times in Revelation that the time was near, not something that was going to take place thousands of years later. The first-century believers understood this. Jesus warned Israel that judgment would come upon them. God brought His judgment down upon them with the total devastation of Jerusalem.

[79]Arthur M. Ogden, The avenging of the Apostles and Prophets: Commentary on Revelation, 2nd ed. (Somerset, KY: Ogden Publications, [1985] 1991, page 320

198

Review

How many times is Armageddon mentioned in the Bible?

Where did the battle take place?

When did it occur?

Why did God allow it to happen?

Does the timing of the battle fit with the rest of Scripture?

Do the symbolic descriptions fit the actual event?

Did John say when this was going to occur?

SECTION FOUR

CHAPTER 13

UNFULFILLED PROPHECIES

What Has Already Happened?

To allow us to see where we are in the Biblical timeline of prophecy, we must look at what prophecy has been clearly explained as having happened already, will never happen, and what is yet to be fulfilled.

In an effort to keep the proper understanding, we must do some reviewing of what we have already written in several of the previous chapters.

The 70th Week of Daniel Has Happened

In the next chapter, we dealt with the misunderstanding of the 70th week of Daniel and the misinterpretation of its application. It has already taken place in history and no future understanding is needed for its fulfillment.

Matthew 24 Has Already Happened

This whole teaching by Jesus was to instruct the disciples as to what was going to take place shortly and dealt specifically with the destruction of Jerusalem and the temple, which did happen with the occupation of Titus in the AD60s and it culminated in the complete destruction of the temple in AD70. It was a terrible time for those who lived then and the city was left utterly desolate. In reading the chapter titled "The Great Tribulation" in section one, it's hard to comprehend the total devastation that was recorded by the Jewish historian Josephus.

No Seven-Year Tribulation Left To Happen

There is no mention in the Bible of a seven-year period of tribulation. It is only in the imagination of the PTDs, however they try and apply this to a future seven-year "Great Tribulation" time span based on Daniel's 70th week. When this is correctly understood as being a past event culminating 3 ½ years after the Lord's crucifixion and when the direction of the message of the Gospel began to be focused on the Gentiles, the fulfillment of Daniel's 70th week was complete.

The actual tribulation event spoken of by our Lord in Matthew 24 had to do with the siege and destruction of Jerusalem that ended with the temple being destroyed in AD70. Therefore, that event has already taken place and the prophecy has been fulfilled.

No Rapture or Lifting Out of The Church

There is no rapture or lifting out of the church or Christians prior to the final, visible and only coming of Christ for His church. In the reading of chapter one of our book titled "Is a rapture of the church indicated in the Bible", it is quite clear that it hasn't happened and is not going to happen.

No 1000-Year Reign of Christ on This Earth

The dispensationalists try to place the 1000-years spoken of in Revelation chapter 20 as some time in the future with the Lord returning from heaven along with His saints to reign on this earth for 1000-years after a seven-year period of tribulation. We took a serious look at the correct interpretation of this passage and it strongly implies an extended period of time between the first time the Lord was here and when He returns. Sometimes these two events are referred to as the first advent and the second advent. This period of time can easily be associated with the church age and it fits very well with the overall view of end-times events. Understanding that this is the only place in Scripture where the millennium or 1000-years is mentioned, it seems quite plausible that is has a symbolic meaning since most of Revelation is written in symbols. In our chapter titled "The Thousand Years" in Section One, we see a clear view of the issues regarding the symbolic nature of the Scripture written by John in Revelation chapter 20.

What's Happening Now?

In light of the fact that we are dealing mainly with events of the past, we should take a pause and look at what is happening now, if it is nothing more than creating awareness of the world that we live in.

Let's look at the moral decay of our world. Just in the last few years, we have seen an enormous attack on Christian ethics and morality. Who would have thought that even just a few years ago we would see such an open acceptance of these things that just a short time ago would have been unthinkable? Here are just a few of them.

Killing babies on demand

Open acceptance of homosexuality

Attack on family values

U.S.A. is no longer a Christian nation

Where Are We? A Review

So are any of these, as well as many attacks on the moral fiber of Christianity, a sign that we are near the end? Not really. As disappointing as these things are, none of the issues mentioned here are necessary and need to happen before the Lord's return. All prophecy and signs have been fulfilled that are needed for the Lord's return. It's just an opportunity to remind my fellow believers where we may be. I have copied a quote from my chapter titled "The Thousand Years" and will repeat it.

"Although this is my own belief, I wish to share it here. Understanding that the 1000-years (indefinite time period) is the church age or the time from the Lord's earthly appearance until near the end, I believe we could be in the time when Satan has been loosed at the end of the thousand years and is attacking believers like never before." This could easily point to the deterioration we are seeing in our world today.

I know there are some who believe this world will get better and return to Christ in large numbers. I just do not see that happening. I would be grateful and excited if it did.

It's not too hard to see that something or someone is deceiving the nations. For clarity of this point, I simply want you to see the possibility of where we may be in the plan and purpose of God. I refuse to set a date or even a season such as what my futurist brothers do. This idea is just for your consideration as you read through this book.

It appears to me that things can and probably will get worse. This is not to be mistaken for the "Great Tribulation" which has already taken place prior to AD70. The way we are going at present, there could easily be a future worsening of our world and its moral values. As Christians, it is important that we stand up for truth and God's righteousness. We must do what the Lord said to His servants in Luke 19:13. We must be busy about spreading the Gospel. It is critical that we follow through and be obedient to the "Great Commission" Jesus spoke about at the end of Matthew chapter 28.

Are There Any Unfulfilled Prophecies?

Understanding that Matthew 24 was fulfilled with the destruction of Jerusalem and the book of Revelation is mainly describing the "Great Tribulation" and the first century church, which has already taken place, are there any additional events that need to happen or any prophecy that needs to be fulfilled before Jesus can come back based on our understanding of the Bible? The answer is an emphatic NO. All necessary prophecy has been fulfilled and no other events or signs need to take place before our Lord returns and receives us into His presence. Let's look at Acts 1:10.

Acts 1:10-11 (NIV)

[10]They were looking intently up into the sky as he was going when suddenly two men dressed in white stood beside them. [11]"Men of Galilee," they said, "why do you stand here looking into the sky? This same Jesus, who has been taken from you into heaven, will come back, in the same way, you have seen him go into heaven."

This passage tells us that when the Lord returns, He will be visible, not a secret coming that some have proposed and not a spiritual coming as some try to teach, but a literal physical coming. He is coming for those of us who are His children and are prepared to meet Him.

John 14:1-3 (NIV)

¹Do not let your hearts be troubled. You believe in God; believe also in me. ²My Father's house has many rooms; if that were not so, would I have told you that I am going there to prepare a place for you? ³And if I go and prepare a place for you, I will come back and take you to be with me that you also may be where I am.

He has gone to prepare a place for us and He is coming back to take us with Him to this prepared place. Please note that wherever He is, it is not on this earth. We are not coming back here to reign with Him for 1000-years as the dispensationalists teach. It is a place that has many mansions and it is ready for us to go there. This passage also tells us that we are going to be where He is. If we are where He is, and it is not here, then it must be someplace else other than this present sinful earth. How exciting it is to know that God made a place that is just for us!

The Promise

Revelation 3:10 (NIV)

¹⁰Since you have kept my command to endure patiently, I will also keep you from the hour of trial that is going to come on the whole world to test the inhabitants of the earth.

Notice that He has promised to keep those who have kept His command. The Greek word used for keep is "tereo" which means to guard against loss or injury. It also implies a fortress or full military lines of apparatus. In other words, He will build a strong fence around those who keep His commands. This is also the same Greek word found in the Lord's prayer to His Father in John 17:11 when He says to keep ("tereo") them through Thy name. He is praying for protection for His disciples after He is gone. That's a powerful picture of how the Lord watches over us. He protects our soul, even if we are in danger physically. We need to fear the Lord and trust in His protection.

Matthew 10:28 (NIV)

²⁸Do not be afraid of those who kill the body but cannot kill the soul. Rather, be afraid of the One who can destroy both soul and body in hell.

He is coming for His church, but in the meantime, He will watch over us and protect us while we are here. Does that mean we will not have any problems? Not at all. As sin still has its consequences, we will still have issues that will cause us troubles. The good news is that He will walk with us and give us the strength to go through them. We're not alone. Let's look at I John 4:4.

1 John 4:4 (NIV)

⁴You, dear children, are from God and have overcome them, because the one who is in you is greater than the one who is in the world.

It is important to understand that God walks with us and is more powerful than the evil one in the world. What a beautiful truth.

He will come in judgment for the sinners and separate them from the Christians. Please look at the chapter again dealing with rapture and especially the Scripture reference in Matthew chapter 13 which states that the good seed and the tares will grow together until the time of harvest. The resurrection of the dead, both sinner and believer, will happen at the same time as noted in John 5:28-29. Please read Daniel 12:2 and Acts 24:15 as they make similar statements to this passage in John.

John 5:28-29 (NIV)

²⁸Do not be amazed at this, for a time is coming when all who are in their graves will hear his voice ²⁹and come out—those who have done what is good will rise to live, and those who have done what is evil will rise to be condemned.

There are other Scriptures that tell us that we will have a new body in that resurrection and rise to live with Christ forever. What a promise!!!

The next thing we need to look at still to happen is found in II Peter 3:10.

II Peter 3:10 (NIV)

¹⁰But the day of the Lord will come like a thief. The heavens will disappear with a roar; the elements will be destroyed by fire, and the earth and everything done in it will be burned up.

Coming like a thief doesn't mean a secret coming but an unexpected one. Do we ever expect a thief to come? So what is Peter saying here? God is going to destroy this whole universe as we know it at His unexpected coming. God's destruction will be total, including the evidence of sin that is part of the terrible past that His people have had to endure while living on this present earth. Now let's look at Revelation 21:1.

Revelation 21:1 (NIV)

¹Then I saw "a new heaven and a new earth," for the first heaven and the first earth had passed away, and there was no longer any sea.

After the entire existing universe is burned up, John tells us there will be a new heaven and a new earth. Actually, you need to look at all of Revelation chapters 21 and 22. Here you will see that John has changed the direction of his writing and recording of his vision. This change focuses on the future and what God has in store for those who are His faithful followers and whose names are found in the book of life.

A Second Chance For The Lost?

Of all the things the dispensationalists teach regarding second coming, the most terrible one is the idea that those who are left behind will have a second chance to be saved. This obviously comes from the idea that many of those who were left behind with this teaching will know the right way but just never did anything about it. Now that they see the Christians are gone they will want to get things right with God before the Lord comes back in seven years to reign on this earth for a thousand years.

Since we have addressed the issue of there not being a rapture with sinners left behind, this false teaching follows the rest of the misinformation that is being taught by them. What a terrible erroneous doctrine being told to the unsaved. The idea that they have a second chance is just simply not Biblical. There is absolutely no Scripture to support such a teaching.

I can't think of a greater false doctrine being taught than this one. Please understand that the time to get saved is now and there is no second chance, no rapture with sinners left behind. The only coming of Christ will be a final one where He will judge both the Christian and the sinner. We have already shown that the entire dispensational teaching is without Bible support, so please don't go down that road of thinking there is a second chance for your eternal destination. So what are we to do until His return?

Matthew 28:19-20 (NIV)

[19]Therefore go and make disciples of all nations, baptizing them in the name of the Father and of the Son and of the Holy Spirit, [20]and teaching them to obey everything I have commanded you. "And surely I am with you always, to the very end of the age."

The command given to the disciples is still valid today. It hasn't changed. The church that isn't making disciples is not following the Lord's command and is probably in the last stages of its existence.

We are to make disciples and spread the Word. We have been given enough truth that it is not an excuse to say that we do not know what we should be doing. Our direction is clear. We are to be witnesses to people about our faith, lead them to the Lord, teach them truth by instructing them in Biblical principles, lead them to a Bible believing church, instruct them regarding the importance of the obedience of baptism and support them in any way we can as new believers and followers of Jesus.

I understand there are many different interpretations on "last days" prophecy and I am certain that I will receive some seriously negative comments by those who disagree with this book. It is not important enough for me to be concerned about the disagreements. I willingly accept that responsibility but am more concerned about getting out the truth of God's Word. It is my hope and desire that reading this book will cause people to dig deeper into the Word of God and commit it to their hearts. If I have done nothing more than encourage you to read, study and absorb His precious Word, then I have done my job. The challenge is to be ready for the Lord's return whenever that may be and to be making disciples while we can. May God bless you.

SECTION FIVE

GLOSSARY OF KEY TERMS

Aaron: He was the older brother of Moses and a prophet of God. Unlike Moses, who grew up in the Egyptian royal court, Aaron remained with his kinsmen in the eastern border-land of Egypt (Goshen). When Moses first confronted the Egyptian king about the Israelites, Aaron served as his brother's spokesman ("prophet") to Pharaoh (Exodus 7:1). Part of the Law (Torah) that Moses received from God at Sinai granted Aaron the priesthood for himself and his male descendants, and he became the first High Priest of the Israelites.

Advent: *Advent* is the period of four Sundays and weeks before Christmas (or sometimes from the 1st December to Christmas Day). It means 'Coming' in Latin. This is the coming of Jesus into the world. Christians use the four Sundays and weeks of **Advent** to prepare and remember the real meaning of Christmas.

Allegory: An allegory is a story in which the characters and/or events are symbols representing other events, ideas, or people. The Bible contains many instances of allegory used to explain spiritual truths or to foreshadow later events. The clearest examples of allegory in Scripture are the parables of Jesus and Revelation. It can be an artistic way of explaining spiritual matters. Much of Revelation is written in an allegorical format.

Allegorical interpretation: Interpreting Scripture in order to find meanings that go beyond the literal interpretation and beneath the surface narrative, making a deeper connection with the reality of Christ. Examples include seeing the crossing of the Red Sea as a symbol or type of baptism or understanding Hagar and Sarah as representatives of the Old and New Covenant (see Galatians 4:21-31). Some of these carry more than one meaning.

A-millennialism: Better known as "realized millennialism" is the belief that the millennium of Revelation 20:1-7 refers to a time of fullness such as the current church age and not to a literal one-thousand-year period of time. While a-millennialists may disagree about what the millennium literally is or will be, they all do agree it will not be a future reign of Christ on this earth. Most who hold this belief understand this to be the time between when Jesus was here the first time, or first advent and His return, or second advent. It is sometimes called the church age.

Antichrist: In the Bible (I John 2:18, 22; 4:3; 2 John 7), a reference to both an anti-Christian religion and possibly a particular individual who will embody that belief at the end of time. More probably a spirit of those who were teaching heresies or false doctrines regarding the Gospel and Christianity.

Apocalypse: From the Greek word meaning an "unveiling" or "revelation". In Christian doctrine, it refers to the unveiling of Jesus Christ as King and Lord that will occur at the end of time at the parousia, or His second coming. This term is found in the opening phrase written in the introduction to the Book of Revelation. (the apocalypse of Jesus Christ)

Apostasy: A rejection of the Christian faith and removal of oneself from the teachings of the Bible. Today it refers to the abandonment of the Christian faith by those who have accepted its truths intellectually. The final apostasy is a great and final rejection of the Christian faith and Jesus toward the end of the world. This is sometimes spoken of as "a great falling away".

Apollos: Apollos was a 1st century Alexandrian Jewish Christian mentioned several times in the New Testament. A contemporary of Paul the Apostle, he played an important role in the early development of the churches of Ephesus and Corinth.

Arethas: Was the leader of the Christian community of Najran in the early 6th century and was executed during persecution the of Christians by the Jewish king Dhu Nuwas in AD523.

Armageddon: Ar-Mageddon is reference to a city (Ar) in proximity to the valley of Meggido or mountain (Har). "City of Megiddo" would be a better translation. You could see the valley and the mountain from Jerusalem. Many battles were fought there.

Book of Mormon: The Mormon Church teaches that the

Bible has been corrupted and does not contain the fullness of the Gospel. This is reflected in one of their Articles of Faith which states: "We believe the Bible to be the word of God **as far as it is translated correctly**". In contrast to the Bible, Mormons believe the Book of Mormon is perfect because it was translated perfectly (miraculously) as reflected in the second half of the same Article of Faith: "...we also believe the Book of Mormon to be the word of God [but without any qualifications as to translation accuracy]". In other words, it has not been corrupted and is without error. The Book of Mormon was written by Joseph Smith and contains many plagiarisms of the King James English (at least 25,000 words) including translational errors. This is strange since the golden plates were supposed to have been buried in the ground by the angel Moroni many centuries before the King James Bible was completed in 1611! The Book of Mormon also contains many errors such as claims of elephants in the Western Hemisphere and advanced metal producing capabilities in America before AD400. The book of Mormon denies the existence of a literal burning hell; it promotes many false teachings such as polytheism (many gods) and baptism for the dead. The Mormon Church has had to continually correct significant errors found in the book in an effort to clarify or answer these known errors. See Mormons in the glossary.

Cult: The two most common teachings of Christian cults are that Jesus was not God and salvation is not by faith alone. They teach Jesus was a created being and therefore not eternal. Denial of the Deity of Christ results in the view that Jesus' death was insufficient to pay for our sins. A denial of salvation by faith alone results in the teaching that salvation is achieved by our own works.

Dispensation: An era of history with a distinct beginning and end. The two major dispensations are the Old and New Covenants. Dispensationalists commonly believe and teach there are seven dispensations in history, each beginning with a test from God and ending with failing the test. (See seven dispensational periods in the glossary.)

Dispensationalism: The theological system formed in the 1830s by Plymouth Brethren leader John Nelson Darby and based on the belief that God is pursuing two different works in history, one involving the Jews, and the other the church. More accurately known as pre-millennial dispensationalism, the movement is a largely American phenomenon. Since the early 1920s and the publication of the *Scofield Reference Bible,* dispensationalism has enjoyed tremendous popularity among Fundamentalist and Evangelical Protestant groups. This teaching has been more recently popularized by books such as Hal Lindsey's *"The Late Great Planet Earth"* and the *"Left Behind"* series by Tim LaHaye.

Dispensationalists: Those who teach the doctrine of dispensationalism. The most popular teaching is a pre-millennial rapture of the church. There are some believers of dispensationalism who have a variety of views on this teaching.

Ecclesiology: Literally, the "study of the church". It is the systematic theological study of the origins, purposes, and nature of the church.

Eschatology: Study of "the last things", especially death, judgment, heaven and hell *(individual eschatology)*. This branch of theology also examines the nature of the kingdom of God, especially as it relates to history, the second coming, the end of time, and the last judgment *(general eschatology)*.

Evangelicalism: A branch of conservative Protestantism characterized by a belief in the centrality and infallibility of the Bible, the need for a personal conversion to Jesus Christ, a strong missionary focus, academic study.

Exegesis: From the Greek, meaning "bringing out the sense". It involves interpreting texts, especially Scripture, and seeking to establish what the authors meant to say and what the text means for Christians today.

First Advent: The first advent happened about 2000 years ago when Jesus came into the world as a baby to live as a man and die for us. When the church celebrates the advent each year, this is what is being remembered.

Fundamentalism: Conservative Protestantism originally formed in the early 1900s in reaction to theological liberalism in mainline Protestant denominations. It is marked by a focus on individual conversion, the sufficiency of Scripture in all aspects of living, a suspicious attitude toward modernity and science, and a negative attitude regarding other evangelicals who do not agree with all of their theology. They are called "secondary separationists" in that they will separate themselves from other evangelical Christians.

Futurism: The belief that all or most of the book of Revelation, as well as many other prophecies, describe future events and provide readers with a detailed explanation of those approaching events. Pre-millennial dispensationalists are futurists, but not all futurists are pre-millennial dispensationalists.

Gnosticism: An ancient heretical movement characterized by a dualism between the material and spiritual realm, with the material realm being evil and the spiritual realm being good. There were many forms of Gnosticism (some claiming to be Christians), but all taught that *gnosis*, or secret knowledge, was the sole means of salvation, not the loving and merciful action of God. Salvation was understood to be the liberation of a person's spiritual essence from the material realm. The New Age movement is a form of Gnosticism and also a group called Christian Science falls into this belief.

Hermeneutics: The science of interpreting and understanding Scripture.

Historic pre-millennialism: An ancient form of pre-millennialism which teaches that at the second coming Jesus Christ will set up an earthly, one-thousand-year reign on earth. Historic pre-millennialism differs from dispensational pre-millennialism in its denial of a rapture event separate from the second coming and in its rejection of the radical distinction between Old Testament Israel and the church.

Historicism: The belief that the book of Revelation provides a prophetic and chronological outline of Christian history. Historicism was embraced by Martin Luther and John Calvin, and a rigid form of it is taught today by such groups as Seventh-Day Adventists. There are some valid elements and insights contained in historicism, and there are others views that benefit from some of them.

Hyper-(or full)-Preterism: A clearly heretical teaching that presumes all prophecy, including the second coming of Christ and the resurrection of Christians, has already been fulfilled.

Idealism: The book of Revelation is not concerned with either past or present events, but depicts spiritual realities, especially the cosmic struggle between God and Satan. Sometimes called the "spiritual" interpretation.

Identity of the beast: The infamous number "666", referred to in the book of Revelation (13:18). Nero is the obvious beast.

Jehovah's Witnesses: Believe in a different Jesus. 1. There is one God in one person, *Make Sure of All Things*, p. 188.

2. There is no Trinity, *Let God be True*, 2nd Ed., pp. 100-101, Should You Believe in the Trinity? p. 7, Watchtower, 2/1/1960, p. 94, Why Do You Believe in the Trinity?

3. The Holy Spirit is a force, not alive, *Reasoning from the Scriptures*, 1985, pp. 406-407.

4. The Holy Spirit is God's impersonal active force, *The Watchtower*, June 1, 1952, p. 24.

5. Jehovah's first creation, his 'only-begotten Son', was used by Jehovah in creating all other things, *Aid to Bible Understanding*, pp. 390-391.

6. Jesus was Michael the archangel who became a man, *The Watchtower*, May 15, 1963, p. 307, *The New World*, 284.

7. Jesus was only a perfect man, not God in flesh, *Reasoning from the Scriptures*, 1985, p. 306.

8. Jesus did not rise from the dead in His physical body, *Awake!* July 22, 1973, p.4.

Kingdom of God/Kingdom of heaven: The final and climactic **reign of God**, ushered in by the Incarnation, growing by means of the church, which is the "seed" of the kingdom. The kingdom will be fully realized at the second coming. The kingdom is a relationship with the God the Father, through Jesus Christ by the power of the Holy Spirit.

Last Judgment: The belief that Christ, at His second coming, will "judge the living and the dead". Jesus spoke of this future event in various ways, using images of wheat and chaff being separated (Matthew 13:24-40, 36-43), the sorting of the good and bad fish (Matthew 13:47-50), the separation of the sheep from the goats (Matthew 25:31-46) and the resurrection of the dead found in John 5:28-29.

Literal interpretation: The meaning conveyed by the words of Scripture and discovered by exegesis, following the rules of sound interpretation. This literal meaning is the basis for all other understanding of Scripture.

Magnum opus: from the Latin meaning "great work", refers to the largest, and perhaps the best, greatest, most popular, or most renowned achievement of an artist or writer.

Mark of the Beast: (Revelation 13:16-17; 16:2; 19:20). Most of the time it is a symbolic (not literal) idea or seal identifying the followers of the beast. It may have been, in some cases, the libellus that Roman citizens were required to carry with them showing allegiance to Caesar. They could not buy or sell without showing it to the authorities.

Melchizedek: First, notice from both Old and New Testaments that this man of mystery was a priest of the Most High God. Notice that Melchizedek was king of Salem. That is the city of Jerusalem. "Salem" comes from the Hebrew word meaning "peace". That would make Melchizedek the "King of Peace" (Hebrews 7:2). The

Hebrew name Melchizedek itself means "King of Righteousness" (Hebrews 7:2). The same individual is mentioned in Psalm 110:4, speaking prophetically of Christ.

Mid-tribulationism: The belief of some dispensationalists that the rapture, the removal of the Christians from the earth, will occur at the midpoint of the seven-year-long tribulation period.

Millenarianism: In general, any belief in a future time of earthly utopia. Within Christianity, it refers to the belief that Jesus will return and establish a thousand-year-long kingdom on earth, especially for Israel.

Millennium: Literally, "a thousand years". Based on Revelation 20:1-10, the meaning of the millennium has been disputed among Christians for many centuries. Dispensationalism believes it refers to a future, earthly reign of Christ, while most Christians believe it represents the current New Testament church age. Figuratively, a long undetermined period of time.

Mormons believe in a different Jesus. First, in Mormon teachings, Jesus is a created being. Therefore, he could not be eternal God or part of an eternal Trinity. Christian apologist Matthew Slick notes several differences regarding Mormonism's view of Jesus:

A. The first spirit to be born in heaven was Jesus (Mormon Doctrine, p. 129).

B. Jesus and Satan are spirit brothers and we were all born as siblings in heaven to them both (Mormon Doctrine, p. 163; Gospel Through the Ages, p. 15).

C. Jesus' sacrifice was not able to cleanse us from all our sins, (murder and repeated adultery are exceptions), (Journal of Discourses, vol. 3, 1856, p. 247).

D. "Therefore we know that both the Father and the Son are in form and stature perfect men; each of them possesses a tangible body . . . of flesh and bones", (Articles of Faith, by James Talmage, p. 38).

Nicene Creed: "I believe in one Lord Jesus Christ, begotten of the Father before all ages, Light of Light, Very God of Very God, begotten, not made, of one essence with the Father, by whom all things were made, who for us men and for our salvation came down from heaven, was incarnate of the Holy Spirit and the Virgin Mary, and was made man; and was crucified also for us under Pontius Pilate, and suffered and was buried; and the third day He rose again from the dead, according to the Scriptures; and ascended into heaven, and sits at the right hand of the Father; and He shall come again with glory to judge the living and the dead, whose Kingdom shall have no end."

Orthodox Christianity: The Orthodox Church is the church founded by Jesus Christ and described throughout the New Testament. All other Christian churches and sects can be traced back historically to it. The word Orthodox literally means "straight teaching" or "straight worship", being derived from two Greek words: orthos, "straight", and Doxa, "teaching" or "worship". As the encroachments of false teaching and division multiplied in early Christian times, threatening to obscure the identity and purity of the church, the term "Orthodox" quite logically came to be applied to it. The Orthodox Church carefully guards the truth against all error and schism, both to protect its flock and to glorify Christ. Jesus Christ is the Second Person of the Trinity, eternally born of the Father. He became a man, and thus He is at once fully God and fully man. His coming to earth was foretold in the Old Testament by the Prophets. Because Jesus Christ is at the heart of Christianity, the Orthodox Church has given more attention to knowing Him than to anything or anyone else.

Preponderance of Evidence: The greater weight of the evidence to decide in favor of one side or the other. This preponderance is based on the more convincing evidence and its probable truth or accuracy, and not on the amount of evidence. Thus, one clearly knowledgeable fact may provide a preponderance of evidence over a dozen so-called facts that may be questionable with less than a clear definition. Preponderance of the evidence is required in a civil case and is contrasted with "beyond a reasonable doubt", which is the most severe test of evidence required to convict in a criminal trial. In layman's terms, a disagreement may be resolved on the clear evidence presented by one side of the argument versus "fuzzy" evidence on the other. It is not the amount of evidence that matters, but the clarity of the evidence presented that's important. What we have endeavored to present in this book is the clarity of the evidence.

PTDs: An abbreviation that simply means pre-tribulation dispensationalists. It refers to those who teach pre-tribulation rapture of the church view of second coming prophecy. It is used many places in this book to simply shorten the long phrase.

Parousia: Literally, "presence". In most cases it refers to the second coming of Jesus Christ and the end of time.

Plagiarize: To take and use the ideas or words of another as one's own: use another's production without crediting the source. There may be similarities in phrases that could possibly make it appear that we have used someone else's material because there are thousands of pages of available material. We have credited the contributors when we have knowingly used their material.

Post-millennialism: The belief that Jesus Christ will return after the church age (symbolic millennium) which will end with the majority of the world being Christianized. It does not see the world getting worse, but it will get better.

Post-tribulationism: The second coming and last judgment will not occur until after a time of tribulation has been endured by the church on earth, right before the second coming.

Pre-millennialism: The belief that the return of Christ will occur prior to the millennium, which is envisioned to be an earthly utopia period, usually a thousand years in length.

Preterism: (Sometimes called Hyper or full preterism.) The belief that all of the events depicted in the prophetic texts of both the Old and New Testaments—especially the Book of Revelation and Matthew 24 have already transpired. Partial or Orthodox Preterists believe most, but not all, of those prophecies, have been fulfilled. Preterists regard the destruction of the Jerusalem Temple in AD70 as a key event in New Testament prophecy.

Pre-tribulationism: The dispensationalists believe the rapture, the secret removal of Christians from the earth, will occur prior to the start of the tribulation period.

Pre-Tribulation Dispensationalists (PTDs): Those who believe and teach the doctrine of rapture, seven-year tribulation and a literal 1000-year reign of Christ on this earth.

Pre-wrath rapture: A variation of the mid-tribulationalism belief. Pre-wrath proponents believe Christians will be raptured out of the tribulation immediately prior to the latter part of the seven-year tribulation where the greatest amount of God's wrath will be poured out upon the earth. The last 3 ½ years is the great wrath of God.

Progressive dispensationalism: A recent version of dispensationalism that seeks to reconcile traditional dispensationalist beliefs with more mainstream Protestant eschatology. The progressives have revised older dispensationalist ideas about the relationship between the church, Old Testament Israel, and the kingdom, and have also advocated methods of Scriptural study that recognize the unity between the Old Testament and New Testament.

Rapture: From the Latin (Vulgate) word meaning "taken up" or "caught up", used in I Thessalonians 4:17. Generally, it refers to the second coming of Christ. However, dispensationalists believe it refers to the sudden, secret, and silent removal of Christians from earth prior to (or in the middle of) the final tribulation.

Reformed: Refers to a branch of Protestantism formed by Calvin, Zwingli, and the Church of England, over against Lutheranism and other forms of Protestantism.

Replacement Theology: Replacement theology is an erroneous teaching that the Christian church has replaced National Israel regarding the plan, purpose, and promises of God. Therefore, many of the promises that God made to National Israel must be spiritualized and fulfilled in the New Testament church. For example, when it speaks of Israel being restored to the land, this really means that the Christian church will be blessed instead. Also, the covenants made with Israel are now being fulfilled in the Christian church. Replacement theology is so deceptive because it rests on half-truths. For instance, the church is the "Israel of God" but not in a replacement sense (Galatians 6:14-16).

Second Advent: The second coming of Christ (sometimes called the Second Advent or the Parousia) is the belief in Christianity regarding a future return of Jesus to earth to judge the sinners and to take His followers to heaven.

Sensationalism: The use of exciting or shocking stories or language at the expense of accuracy, in order to provoke public interest or excitement.

Sense of Scripture: The different meanings that a biblical passage conveys. The two major senses of Scripture are the literal and the spiritual, the "latter being subdivided into the allegorical, moral, and anagogical senses".

Seven Dispensational Periods: Theologies between the Old Testament and the New Testament. Its name comes understood in light of from the fact that it sees Biblical history as best a series of dispensations in the Bible. Most dispensationalists cite seven dispensations although this is not a critical or foundational factor to the theology:

- the dispensation of innocence (Gen 1:1–3:7), prior to Adam's fall

- of conscience (Gen 3:8–8:22), Adam to Noah

- of government (Gen 9:1–11:32), Noah to Abraham

- of patriarchal rule (Gen 12:1–Exod 19:25), Abraham to Moses

- of the Mosaic Law (Exod 20:1–Acts 2:4), Moses to Christ

- of grace (Acts 2:4–Rev. 20:3), the longest dispensation is the current church age

- of a literal, earthly 1,000-year Millennial Kingdom that has yet to come but soon will (Rev 20:4–20:6)

Tacitus: Publius (or **Gaius**) **Cornelius Tacitus**: (AD56 – after 117) was a senator and a historian of the Roman Empire. The surviving portions of his two major works— the *Annals* and the *Histories*—examine the reigns of the Roman Emperors Tiberius, Claudius, Nero, and those who reigned in the Year of the Four Emperors(AD69). These two works span the history of the Roman Empire from the death of Augustus in AD14 to the years of the First Jewish/Roman War in AD70. There are several substantial gaps in the surviving texts, including a gap in the *Annals* that is four books long.

The Great Tribulation: Dispensationalists see this as a future period of trial and testing of the Jews after the church has been raptured or lifted out. It is viewed as the final conflict between Satan, the antichrist, and false prophet resulting in the triumphant return of Jesus Christ after seven years to reign on this earth 1000-years. This issue is addressed at length in our chapter called "The Great Tribulation".

Theological Terminology: Use of Biblical words or study that may need further definition or explanation.

Tribulation (or Jacob's trouble): More than likely this is the 42-month period when Jerusalem was occupied by the Romans and the temple was destroyed. It was a terrible time for those living in Jerusalem with a lot of bloodshed and persecution when this occurred. We have addressed this terrible time and included a great deal of Josephus' (who was a Jewish historian) vivid writings.

Two Witnesses: The Two Witnesses are the 'Two Olive Trees' of Rev. 11:4, fulfilling the prophecy of Zechariah 4: 1-14 which looked forward to the mission of the church. The Two Olive Trees of Zechariah 4 are closely associated with the Seven Candlesticks. The Seven Candlesticks appear in Revelation 1 to 3 where they are clearly shown to refer to the church. The Two Olive Trees and the Two Witnesses represent the church. Here the church is shown to be the most important piece of this puzzle by being a witness of the Gospel. The Two Olive Trees are the Two Witnesses, which are first represented by Elijah and Elisha and then later by John the Baptist and Jesus. The continuation is realized whenever and wherever Christians preach the Gospel. So we are all part of the mission of the Two Witnesses. This is the proper Biblical approach and does not separate Revelation from the rest of God's Word. It is important to realize that virtually all of the Book of Revelation is symbolic and the underlying truth of those symbols must be found in other prophetic Scriptures. There is no need to search for future individuals to fit this passage because we, as witnesses, are responsible to carry the message and fulfill the Great Commission.

Veil: During the lifetime of Jesus, the holy temple in Jerusalem was the center of Jewish religious life. The temple was the place where animal sacrifices were carried out and worship according to the Law of Moses was followed faithfully. Hebrews 9:1-9 tells us that in the temple a veil separated the Holy of Holies, the earthly dwelling place of God's presence, from the rest of the temple where men dwelt. This signified that man was separated from God by sin (Isaiah 59:1-2). Only the high priest was permitted to pass beyond this veil once each year (Exodus 30:10; Hebrews 9:7) to enter into God's presence for all of Israel and make atonement for their sins (Leviticus 16). Solomon's temple was 30 cubits high (1 Kings 6:2), but Herod had increased the height to 40 cubits, according to the writings of Josephus, a first-century Jewish historian. There is uncertainty as to the exact measurement of a cubit, but it is safe to assume that this veil was somewhere near 60 feet high. An early Jewish tradition says that the veil was about four inches thick, but the Bible does not confirm that measurement. The book of Exodus teaches that this thick veil was fashioned from blue, purple and scarlet material and fine twisted linen. The size and thickness of the veil make the events occurring at the moment of Jesus' death on the cross so much more momentous. "And when Jesus had cried out again in a loud voice, he gave up his spirit. At that moment, the curtain of the temple was torn in two from top to bottom" (Matthew 27:50-51a). So, what do we make of this? What significance does this torn veil have for us today? Above all, the tearing of the veil at the moment of Jesus' death dramatically symbolized that His sacrifice, the shedding of His own blood, was a sufficient atonement for sins. It signified that now the way into the Holy of Holies was open for all people, for all time, both Jew and Gentile because Jesus is our High Priest.

Whore of Babylon: Taken from Revelation 17:5 which has been applied to various entities throughout history. The early church fathers believed it referred to secular Rome. The Protestant reformers and many fundamentalists today identify the whore of Babylon as the Catholic Church and the antichrist being the final super-man-pope. It is our belief that this is apostate Israel and her great falling away from the truth of God.

Appendix 1:

Eschatology Is The Doctrine Of Last Things

Eschatology is the doctrine of last things. What is to happen before, during, and after the second coming of the Lord Jesus Christ? There are four major systems of eschatology each with subsystems that may carry a particular view into different interpretations.

Each of the four major systems of eschatology all claim to be the most scriptural. We can all cite our heroes who believe as we do or rather we believe as they do. Over the last several years I have attempted to be objective in my study of eschatology. When I first developed an interest in the doctrine of last things I had mainly been taught a pre-tribulation rapture of the believer approach in both the church and at Bible College. Then a seven-year tribulation period was to follow. After that was a 1000-year reign of Christ on this earth with His saints. This just simply didn't seem to fit the Word of God and I soon learned that much of this teaching was assumptions with very little actual Bible to support it. I also had a father who did not believe this teaching and he shared with me what he believed was a better understanding of the second advent sequence of events. An advantage to being taught two different systems gave me an opportunity to compare them to each other. Too often the basis for holding to a singular system of eschatology is: "That is what I have always been taught."

234

It is then a matter of pride to insist that what we first learned must be correct. One of the marks of a believer is that he is teachable [meek] and remain so as long as he lives. Other men decide that eschatology is not important at all and thus have adopted none of the accepted views, except to trust that it will all "pan out". They are "Panmillennialists". Please understand the subtle humor here with this statement.

Eschatology is important because your system of eschatology will necessarily interpret Scripture for you. E.g., when you read Romans 11:26, "And so all Israel will be saved" and, of course, you know who or what "Israel" is, then you will interpret to whom Paul is referring based on your eschatology. The man who has no consistent eschatology will be inconsistent in his understanding of the entire Bible.

"Never underestimate the power of a preconceived notion." – Charles Alexander

Here is a very simple description of the four major views that only states what is to me "the bottom line". I have deliberately omitted the hyper or total-Preterism view which is [all prophecies were fulfilled at the destruction of Jerusalem in AD70] simply because I do not accept it with a lot of credibility. It is not my purpose to define each system in detail, including my own. I do give great credence to "partial preterism" which states that some end time prophecies have been fulfilled while others are yet to happen.

First: **Dispensationalism**: The millennium or one thousand years mentioned in Revelation chapter 20 is in the future. The current most popular view and to me the most extreme view of pre-millennialism is dispensationalism. This view of last things says that the nation of Israel (Israel after the flesh) is the focus of the Bible. The Bible begins and ends with ethnic Israel as a nation. The church is an afterthought, or a "parenthesis". Israel is National Israel and Israel will never be part of the church. There are two ways to be saved, be born a Jew, or to be a Christian. The church and Israel are two separate entities and the one is never part of the other. The Nation of Israel will be restored at the return of Christ and Christ will reign as King on the earth over a literal kingdom for a literal 1000-years. Many Old Testament prophecies of a land are not completely fulfilled in the Old Testament nor in the church in a heavenly Jerusalem. They are reserved for the millennium. The Old Testament takes precedence over the New Testament. The church is "raptured" or lifted out of this world at the return of Christ to be forever separated from Israel. The temple will be rebuilt in Jerusalem and animal sacrifices will once again be offered. Judaism is restored in all its former glory. To be fair, dispensationalism has been modified in recent years but the current popular version is pretty close to what is described above. We will address these issues throughout the book.

Second: **Historic Pre-millennialism**: The millennium is in the future. National Israel will be restored at the return of Christ and Christ will reign for a literal 1000-years on earth. Jews will be saved because they are Jews although it will be through the belief of the Gospel. The Jews thus saved will become part of the church. This differs from dispensationalism as historic pre-millennialism proposes the saved Jews will not be separate from the church.

Third: **Post-millennialism**: The millennium is in the future. There will be an approximate 1000-years of peace and a strong Christian influence in the world before the return of Christ at the end of time including a great spiritual revival. The Jews have a special place in redemptive history because they are Jews.

Fourth: **A-millennialism**: The millennium is now. Instead of a-millennialism, I prefer to use the term "realized millennialism". We are now in the millennial reign of Christ with the tares growing among the wheat, description found in Matthew chapter 13. The "a" in a-millennialism means no millennium, which is a misnomer. Those who hold to a-millennialism believe that the "millennium" is the period of time between the first advent or coming of Christ and His second coming. Christ the King reigns now in this present age in heaven. Therefore realized millennialism is a more correct description and could also be called the church age. There is no rapture or lifting out of the church prior to the end of the age. It is also understood that the devil will be loosed for a season near the end of the church age shortly before the Lord's second coming.

There are only two ages in the Bible – this present age and the age to come (these are biblical terms). There are two "Israels" in Scripture. There is **National Israel**, which has been rejected by God, and the "**Israel of God**" which is the church. The focus of the Bible is on the church as they are redeemed in Christ as individuals. God saves sinners through the means of the Gospel in all of human history. Before the institution of the local church there were individuals from every race and tribe who were called by God. There is nothing to follow the church when Christ returns. God's elect will be with Him in glory for eternity. Unbelievers are forever in hell. The New Testament interprets the Old.

Some, who hold to a-millennialism, e.g. Dr. Martyn Lloyd-Jones, believe that vast numbers of Jews will be saved through the Gospel at the end of the age. I have no problem with vast numbers of Jews, or anyone else, being saved as individuals but I do have a problem with the idea that Jews will be saved because of their birth certificate. Just being born a Jew will not save you.

The conclusion: The Lord Jesus Christ in Matthew 21:43 says:

Matthew 21:43 (NIV)

⁴³Therefore I tell you that the kingdom of God will be taken away from you and given to a people who will produce its fruit.

And the "kingdom of God is at hand", not yet future. The Jews forfeited any and all claims to the kingdom because of unbelief. The "nation" that bears the fruit of the kingdom of God is the church, the Israel of God.

When John the Baptist, referring to Jesus of Nazareth, proclaimed, "Behold the Lamb of God who takes away the sin of the world," he was not only pointing to the Messiah but he was announcing the end of Judaism and the old covenant.

My case for a-millennialism or realized millennialism is as follows. (I will use a-millennial and realized millennium interchangeably. The more correct phase is "realized millennium").

How do I make my argument for realized millennialism? Rather than tackle what are to me all of the faults of the other major views I will follow some lines of thought that each led me to realized millennialism. Most of my comparisons are between dispensationalism and a-millennialism although much of the argument can also apply to historic pre-millennialism.

1. The focus of the Bible is the church and not National Israel.
2. God deals with individuals and not nations in the matter of eternal salvation.
3. God has always included the Gentiles in the number of His elect.
4. There are two Israels in Scripture.
5. The covenant promises in the Old Testament have been fulfilled, forfeited, or made to Christ and His church.
6. The New Testament interprets the Old Testament. (This is critical to the understanding of New Testament prophecy.)

I cannot emphasize enough the importance of these six points above.

Principles Of Bible Interpretation

It is essential that you have a solid system of Bible interpretation or you will be "tossed back and forth by the waves, and blown here and there by every wind of teaching and by the cunning and craftiness of people in their deceitful scheming" (Ephesians 4:14).

Either the focus of the entire Bible is on Israel (the Jews) or the focus of the Bible is on the church. So is the Bible mainly about the Jews or is the Bible mainly about the church? Of course the Bible is about both the Jews and the church, but what is its end objective, its focus?

Is the Old Testament about the Jews and the New

Testament about the church and will the Jews once more be prominent in the grand scheme of things? Or is the Bible about the church in both the Old Testament and the New Testament?

You must understand that these two views on the focus of the Bible are so radically different that there is really no room for compromise. One is correct and the other one is wrong. They cannot both be correct.

The Jews say the focus of the Bible is on the claim that their view is the most literal interpretation of the Bible. The idea that says the focus of the Bible is on the church is said to be a more spiritual interpretation.

However, it is not really accurate to assign "more literal" or "more spiritual" to either view regarding the focus of the Bible because proponents of both views take what they consider to be literal as literal and spiritualize the text when it suits their method of interpretation. Neither view is more accurate based solely on who says what is literal and what is literary. All Scripture must be kept in context and interpreted in light of all Scripture, not just one verse by itself. This is what I am trying to do in the writing of this book.

Dispensationalism claims to be the most literal interpretation of the Bible and is embodied in the popular *"Left Behind"* series of books by Tim LaHaye. In the 1970s it was *"The Late Great Planet Earth"* that was all the rage.

The view that says the focus of the Bible is on the

church, and is said to be more spiritual, is called a-millennialism.

In my opinion, there are not many books written about the more spiritual view of interpretation. This view is not sensational. We know that sensationalism sells books, but we felt the need to write the clear reading of prophecy rather than sensationalize it.

A-millennialism has no "secret rapture" with Christians flying on airplanes suddenly disappearing. There is only one general resurrection of the dead.

John 5:28-29 (NIV)

[28]Do not be amazed at this, for a time is coming when all who are in their graves will hear his voice [29]and come out—those who have done what is good will rise to live, and those who have done what is evil will rise to be condemned.

There is no third or fourth temple with renewed animal sacrifices. There is simply this present age and the age to come, and that's it. The Bible does not mention another temple being rebuilt after the second temple was destroyed in AD70.

There is much more involved in the intricacies of dispensationalism in addition to what I will point out, but these points are essential to that system of interpretation. I personally do not feel that God would have the authors write in such a way as to cause men to be confused.

I Corinthians 14:33 (NIV)

³³For God is not a God of disorder but of peace—as in all the congregations of the Lord's people.

The KJV translates the word disorder as confusion. It is man that confuses God's word by trying to read into it things that simply are not there. The confusion is in twisting the Scripture to their own biased thinking.

First: If dispensationalism falls short in any one of these principles of interpretation, its entire system of interpretation will crumble. Understanding this, when we deal with the rapture, the tribulation and the 1000-year reign, this will cast serious doubt on the whole approach of the dispensationalist view. Their view depends totally on the whole series of events.

And so the "First Principle of Interpretation" is on how you view the focus of the Bible. Is it the Jews or the church? The dispensationalists say the focus is the Jews while others say the Jews are a part of the entire church from Genesis to Revelation. (see our chapter on "When Did the Church Start")

Secondly: the New Testament interprets the Old Testament. Dispensationalism says that the New Testament does not interpret the Old Testament and that all of the Old Testament prophecies concerning the Jews were not literally fulfilled in the Old Testament but must be literally fulfilled in a time that is yet in the future. This time yet to come includes the seven years of tribulation and the "millennium" or a literal 1000-year reign of Christ on this earth.

Thirdly: The true church is found in both the Old Testament and the New Testament. Dispensationalism does not allow that the church is found in the Old Testament. By the "church" I mean all Gentiles and Jews who are true followers of God and who believe the same Gospel that we preach today. I do not mean the visible church organization as it was instituted on the Day of Pentecost in Acts 2.

Dispensationalism makes a fixed and firm separation between National Israel and the church. This separation between Israel and the church, according to dispensationalism will be forever.

Fourth: Dispensationalism recognizes two methods of salvation, one for the Jews and one for the church. Dispensationalism claims that salvation is by grace but it insists that God will save the Jews because they are Jews. This is a general statement, as not all Dispensationalists agree with this nor do they all agree with each other on several points of dispensationalism. In fact it is sometimes hard to pin them down as to what they believe about certain Scriptures. This can make it somewhat difficult to discuss issues with them until you can know for certain what they individually believe.

244

E.g., Roman Catholicism also says that salvation is by grace. But "grace", according to the Roman Catholic teaching, is only to be obtained through the sacraments of the church. So they can call it "grace" but it amounts to something that you must do or be in order to be saved. Remember that salvation is grace plus nothing. We cannot work our way to heaven by anything we do.

There are highly respected men of God who hold diverse views of eschatology.

Eschatology is not, at least it is not to me, a test of fellowship. I have many Christian friends who believe in a pre-tribulation rapture of the church. We just respectfully disagree with each other.

A test of fellowship is something over which you would part company, or break fellowship. One example of a test of fellowship for me is the Deity of Christ. Anyone who denies that Jesus Christ of Nazareth is God is not yet a believer and cannot possibly participate in Christian fellowship.

What I am presenting here is not simply repeating what another man has written. What I believe is based on an objective examination of eschatology over several years of Bible study.

Salvation is by God's grace and He saves individuals as individuals. The nations (Gentiles) have always been included as God's children if they followed Him as individuals. Salvation was not for the Jews only.

Romans 9:23-26 (NIV)

²³"What if he did this to make the riches of his glory known to the objects of his mercy, whom he prepared in advance for glory— ²⁴even us, whom he also called, not only from the Jews but also from the Gentiles? ²⁵As he says in Hosea: "I will call them 'my people' who are not my people; and I will call her 'my loved one' who is not my loved one," ²⁶and, "In the very place where it was said to them, 'You are not my people, there they will be called 'children of the living God.'"

There has always been a "remnant" of Israel included in God's elect. There never was a generation of Jews who were all saved simply because they were born Jews.

Romans 9:27-29 (NIV)

²⁷Isaiah cries out concerning Israel: "Though the number of the Israelites be like the sand by the sea, only the remnant will be saved.²⁸For the Lord will carry out his sentence on earth with speed and finality." ²⁹It is just as Isaiah said previously: "Unless the Lord Almighty had left us descendants, we would have become like Sodom, we would have been like Gomorrah."

Our salvation is and always has been that we are saved by grace through faith, not by works. (Eph. 2:8-9) The keeping of the law in the Old Testament was an obedience issue and pointed to the future sacrifice of Jesus on the cross. Please take time to read the entire 11th chapter of Hebrews. You will see that all of these Old Testament people mentioned in this passage were saved by faith.

The mystery of the ages is not if there would be a church but rather the make-up of the church. The mystery that has been revealed is that the true church has always been made of Gentiles and Jews. The church is the total number of the redeemed and includes only individuals who were saved by grace, one at a time.

Appendix 2:

Worship of the Beast
Revelation 13:4 (NIV)

⁴People worshiped the dragon because he had given authority to the beast, and they also worshiped the beast and asked, "Who is like the beast? Who can wage war against it?"

In chapter 8 we briefly addressed the worship of the beast. Let's look at more information regarding this subject. The beast of Revelation that John wrote about was both generic (Rome) and specific (Nero). So let's first look at the generic or Rome and then emperor worship.

Julius Caesar

"Emperor worship had its roots in the reign of Julius Caesar, the first ruler of the Roman Empire."[80] He was described by an inscription at Ephesus discovered which read "god manifest and common savior of the life of man".[81] After Julius' death, a twenty foot high marble statue was set up to honor him and Suetonius notes that "at the foot of this they continued for a long time to sacrifice, make vows, and settle some of their disputes by an oath in the name of Caesar".[82]

---

[80] The Beast of Revelation, Ken Gentry , American Vision Powder Springs GA. Page 74
[81] James J.L. Ratton, *The Apocalypse of John* (London: R. and T. Washbourne, 1912) 48. See Dio Cassius 47:18:33
[82] Suetonius, Julius 88

Octavian/Augustus

"The empire's second ruler, Augustus, forbad divine worship to himself in Rome,[83] but Tacitus and Suetonius wrote that he sanctioned his worship and erection of altars elsewhere."[84] Scullard writes regarding Octavian (i.e. Augustus):

"In one respect Octavian had long been unique: since 42BC and the consecrations of Divus Julius he had been the son of a god, "Divi filius". After Actium his birthday was celebrated as a public holiday; libations were poured in his honor at public and private banquets; from 29BC his name was added to those of the gods in hymns; two years later he received the title of Augustus; his Genius, perhaps in 12BC, was inserted in official oaths between the names of Jupiter and the Di Penates; in AD13 an altar was dedicated by Tiberius in Rome to the Numen Augustus."[85]

Tiberius Caesar

In Matthew 22:15-22, Jesus is defining who they should worship. Jesus is implying here that Tiberius who ruled from AD14 to AD37, should not be worshipped.

---

[83] He hated the title of "Dominius" ("Lord") because he preferred to be known as governor of free men rather than master of slaves.
[84] Suetonius *Augustus* 52-53, Tacitus , *Annals* 1:10
[85] Scullard, *Gracchi* , 242

Matthew 22:15-22 (NIV)

15Then the Pharisees went out and laid plans to trap him in his words. 16They sent their disciples to him along with the Herodians. "Teacher," they said, "we know that you are a man of integrity and that you teach the way of God in accordance with the truth. You aren't swayed by others, because you pay no attention to who they are. 17Tell us then, what is your opinion? Is it right to pay the imperial tax 86 to Caesar or not?" 18But Jesus, knowing their evil intent, said, "You hypocrites, why are you trying to trap me? 19Show me the coin used for paying the tax." They brought him a denarius, 20and he asked them, "Whose image is this? And whose inscription?" 21"Caesar's," they replied. Then he said to them, "So give back to Caesar what is Caesar's, and to God what is God's." 22When they heard this, they were amazed. So they left him and went away.

"At Tiberius's death, eleven cities of Asia struggled for the honor of erecting a temple in his memory."[87] "The senate finally awarded the temple to Smyrna",[88] one of the seven cities to which John addressed in Revelation.

---

[86] Matthew 22:17 A special tax levied on subject peoples, not on Roman citizens

[87] Herbert B. Workman, *Persecution in the Early Church* (Oxford: Oxford University Press, [1906] (1980), 39ff.

[88] Edward C. Selwyn, *The Christian Prophets & the Prophetic Apocalypse* (London: Macmillan, 1900, 123

250

Gaius ("Caligula") Caesar

"The fourth ruler of the Roman Empire was Gaius Caesar, also known as by his nickname "Caligula". Gaius was clearly a madman possessed with the conviction of his own deity. He placed the head of his own statue on that of Jupiter, had himself saluted as Jupiter, and had temples erected to himself."[89]

"Gaius puffed himself up with pride, not only saying, but actually thinking he was a god."[90]

Philo records the following, "Gaius has ordered a colossal statue of himself to be erected in the holy of holies, having his own name inscribed upon it with the title of Jupiter."[91] Only his death prevented this from happening, which would have obviously caused a war with the Jews.

"Caligula began to go further than ever before, much farther than either of the two previous emperors, in authorizing his own deification to take effect immediately while he was still alive. What Caligula now arranged at Rome was something quite unprecedented, the establishment of two temples of his own godhead, one erected from his own resources and the other at state expense by decree of the senate."[92]

---

[89] Suetonius, *Caligula* 21
[90] Philo, *Embassy to Gaius*, 162
[91] Philo, *Embassy to Gaius*, 774
[92] Grant, *The Twelve Caesars*, 121-22

Claudius Caesar

The fifth and immediate ruler before Nero was Claudius Caesar. Even while he was alive a temple was erected to him at Colchester.[93] "Claudius's new foundation included a large and sumptuous temple dedicated to his own divinity."[94] Grant further made this statement: "writers were permitted to speak of his sacred hands and duties, and even described him as 'our god Caesar'."[95]

Summary Of The First Five Emperors

"In the first century AD, all of the emperors claimed divinity for themselves. The emperors after Augustus especially promoted the cult of the emperor."[96]

"Christians living in the seven cities mentioned in the book of Revelation probably found the imperial cult an objectionable social, religious institution, but it was just as objectionable under Claudius as Domitian. Change in emperors throughout the first century did not affect the presence of the cult in Asia. Five of the seven cities had imperial altars (all but Philadelphia and Laodicea), six had imperial temples (all but Thyatria), and five had imperial priest (all but Philadelphia and Laodicea)."[97]

---

[93] Workman, *Persecution*, 40
[94] Grant, *Twelve Caesars*, 139
[95] ibid
[96] Kurt Aland, *A History of Christianity* (Philadelphia: Fortress, 1985) 1:18
[97] Thompson, *the Book of Revelation*, 159

"The churches of the Book of Revelation were located geographically, organizationally, and culturally where the imperial cult was most heavily distributed."[98]

Nero Caesar

Now that we have been able to establish that the first five rulers of Rome (the generic beast) all set themselves up as gods by building temples, altars, images, and statues, let's take a look at Nero. Since it has been clearly shown that he fits the description of the specific beast in Revelation, it remains to be seen if he too led the people to believe he was a god.

"Nero was surely the most notorious Roman emperor of the first century, excelling both the insane Caligula and the paranoid Domitian in notoriety. He was jealously vain in his proud appreciation of his own artistic talents. How could such a vain character resist the glory afforded by the emperor cult? As a matter of historical record, he did not."[99] "There were coins minted with the image of Nero's head radiating the light of the sun."[100]

"Seneca convinced Nero that he was destined to become the very revelation of the divine Augustus and of the god Apollo."[101] "All of this was more than pomp and

---

[98] Thompson, *The Book of Revelation*, 160
[99] Ken Gentry, *The Beast of Revelation*, American Vision Powder Springs GA. Page 80
[100] ibid
[101] Seneca, On Clemency 1:16: Apocolocyntosis (or Pumpkinification) 4:15-35

show: Nero strove with deadly seriousness to play the role of Augustus and Apollo politically, the former primarily from AD54 to AD61 and the latter from AD62 to AD68."[102] "Remarkably, eastern provincial coins hailed Nero's mother (Agrippina) "as goddess and parent of a god".[103]

Nero was actually worshipped, for there were inscriptions found in Ephesus which called him "Almighty God" and "Savior".[104] He was also referred to as "God and Savior" in an inscription at Salamis, Cyprus".[105]

His influence became stronger, in time, as his images and features began to appear in many places. "Nero deified his child by Poppaea and then Poppaea herself after their deaths. All this was far removed from the modest attitude of Augustus."[106] "Caligula and Nero, the only two of the Julio-Claudians who were direct descendants of Augustus, demanded divine honors while they were still alive."[107]

In his publication of "Roman History" on Nero, page 62:5:2, Dio Cassius relates the incident of Tiridates, King of Armenia, in AD66, paid reverence to the images

---

[102] Bo Reicke, *The New Testament Era: The World of the bible from 500 BC to AD 100* (Philadelphia: Fortress, 1968) 70

[103] Michael Grant, *Nero* (New York: Dorest, 1970),31

[104] Ratton, *Apocalypse*, 48

[105] Smallwood, *Documents Illustrating the Principates*, 142

[106] Scullard, *Gracchi*, 371

[107] Joseph Ward Swain, *The Harper History of Civilization* (New York: Harper, 1958), 1:229

of Nero and after sacrificing to the images, took off his crown and set it upon the images. He further bowed before Nero, calling him, "my god" and saying "I worship thee".[108] By this action, the king actually worshipped the image of the beast prophesied in Revelation.

"During the Roman civil wars, begun with the death of Nero in June AD68, the emperor Vitellius even offered sacrifices to the spirit of the deceased Nero."[109]

The evidence presented here regarding emperor worship shows we are right on target in designating the Roman empire as the generic beast and Nero the specific beast which John wrote about in Revelation.

---

[108] Dio Cassius, *Roman History* 62:5:2
[109] Ken Gentry, The Beast of Revelation, American Vision Powder Springs GA. Page 84

Appendix 3:

Early Date Advocates

Here are just a few of the Biblical scholars who believe that Revelation was written before AD70.

Jay E. Adams (1966)

"...[the temple still standing in Revelation 11:1 is] unmistakable proof that Revelation was written before 70 A.D." (*The Time is at Hand*, p. 68).

"The Revelation was written to a persecuted church about to face the most tremendous onslaught it had ever known. It would be absurd (not to say cruel) for John to write a letter to persons in such circumstances which not only ignores their difficulties, but reveals numerous details about events supposed to transpire hundreds of years in the future during a seven year tribulation period at the end of the church age." (*The Time is at Hand*, p. 49)

"It is to remain unsealed *because* 'the time is at hand'. That is, its prophecies are about to be fulfilled. The events which it predicts do not pertain to the far distant future, but they are soon to happen. The message is for this generation, not for some future one." (*The Time is at Hand*, p. 51)

256

Adam Clarke (1837)

(On **Revelation 1:7**) "By this the Jewish People are most evidently intended, and therefore the whole verse may be understood as predicting the destruction of the Jews; and is a presumptive proof that the Apocalypse was written before the final overthrow of the Jewish state." (Clarke commentary on the Bible)

John Albert Bengel (1687-1752): The Father of Modern Biblical Scholarship

"Bengel has said much on these points, but to very little purpose; the word in the above place seems to signify delay simply, and probably refers to the long-suffering of God being ended in reference to Jerusalem; for I all along take for probable that this book was written previously to the destruction of that city." (Revelation 10)

Henry Cowles (1871)

"The conclusion to which I am brought after much investigation is that the historic testimony for the Domitian date is largely founded on a misconception of the passage from Irenaeus, and as a whole is by no means so harmonious, so ancient, and so decisive, as to overrule and set aside the strong internal evidence for the earlier date. I am compelled to accept the age of Nero as the true date of this writing." (**The Book of Revelation**)

F.W. Farrar (1886)

"...there can be no reasonable doubt respecting the (early) date of the Apocalypse." (*The Early Days of Christianity*; NY, NY: A.L. Burt, 1884; p. 387)

"We cannot accept a dubious expression of the Bishop of Lyons as adequate to set aside an overwhelming weight of evidence, alike external and internal, in proof of the fact that the Apocalypse was written, at the latest, soon after the death of Nero." (*The Early Days of Christianity*; NY, NY: A.L. Burt, 1884; p. 408)

"The reason why the early date and mainly contemporary explanation of the book is daily winning fresh adherents among unbiased thinkers of every Church and school, is partly because it rests on so simple and secure a basis, and partly because no other can compete with it. It is indeed the only system which is built on the plain and repeated statements and indications of the Seer himself and the corresponding events are so closely accordant with the symbols as to make it certain that this scheme of interpretation is the only one that can survive." (*The Early Days of Christianity*; NY, NY: A.L. Burt, 1884; p. 434)

Ken Gentry (1989)

"My confident conviction is that a solid case for a Neronic date for Revelation can be set forth from the available evidences, both internal and external. In fact, I would lean toward a date after the outbreak of the Neronic persecution in late AD64 and before the declaration of the Jewish war in early AD67. A date in either AD65 or early AD66 would seem most suitable." (*Before Jerusalem Fell* (Tyler, TX: ICE, 1989), 336.)

"John emphasizes his anticipation of the soon occurrences of his prophecy by *strategic placement* of these time references. He places his boldest time statements in both the introduction and conclusion to Revelation. It is remarkable that so many recent commentators have missed it literally coming and going! The statement of expectancy is found three times in the first chapter – twice in the first three verses: Revelation 1:1,3,19. The same idea is found four times in his concluding remarks: Revelation 22:6,7,12,20. *It is as if John carefully bracketed the entire work to avoid any confusion.*" (*The Beast of Revelation*; Tyler, TX; ICE, 1982; p. 21-22).

"Think of it: If these words in these verses do not indicate that John expected the events to occur soon, *what words could John have used to express such*? How could he have said it more plainly?" (*The Beast of Revelation*; Tyler, TX; ICE, 1982; p. 24).

"It seems indisputably clear that the book of Revelation must be dated in the reign of Nero Caesar, and consequently *before* his death in June, A.D.68. He is the sixth king; the short-lived rule of the seventh king (Galba) "has not yet come." (*Before Jerusalem Fell* (Tyler, TX: ICE, 1989; 158.)

Ovid Need Jr. (2001)

"I will say in opening that Revelation chapter eleven almost requires that the date of the book be pre AD70, for there the temple and altar are still standing, as well as the city where our Lord was crucified, v. 8. (*International Bible Encyclopedia*, s.v. Revelation, book of. 1917.)

Admittedly, there are good arguments for both an early and a later date of the Revelation. However, I believe Biblical evidence requires an early date, before AD70. As an introductory statement, let me mention that prophecy is from the time it is written, NOT FROM THE TIME IT IS READ.

A pre AD70 date would make the purpose of the Revelation the same as was Isaiah's prophecy -- that is, to see the faithful people of God through the extremely difficult times ahead as their then known world was going to be shaken to its very foundation by the judgment of God against Babylon." (Revelation: Date, Time and Purpose)

Ernest Renan

"It may be that, after the crisis of the year 68 (the date of the Apocalypse) and of the year 70 (the destruction of Jerusalem), the old Apostle, with an ardent and plastic spirit, disabused of the belief in a near appearance of the Son of Man in the clouds, may have inclined towards the ideas that he found around him, of which several agreed sufficiently well with certain Christian doctrines. " (Life of Jesus)

R.C. Sproul (1998)

"If the book of Revelation was written after the destruction of Jerusalem and the temple, it seems strange that John would be silent about these cataclysmic events. Granted this is an argument from silence, but the silence is deafening. Not only does Revelation not mention the temple's destruction as a past event, it frequently refers to the temple as still standing. This is seen clearly in Revelation 11 ...Gentry gives impressive evidence to support this conclusion." (*Last Days*, pp.147-149)

Moses Stuart (1845)

"The testimony in respect to the matter before us is evidently successive and dependent, not coetaneous and independent". (1:282. 81)

"If now the number of the witnesses were the only thing which should control our judgment in relation to the question proposed, we must, so far as external evidence is concerned, yield the palm to those who fix upon the time of Domitian. But a careful examination of this matter shows, that the whole concatenation of witnesses in favor of this position hangs upon the testimony of Irenaeus, and their evidence is little more than a mere repetition of what he has said. Eusebius and Jerome most plainly depend on him; and others seem to have had in view his authority, or else that of Eusebius." (Ibid. 2:269)

"I say this, with full recognition of the weight and value of Irenaeus's testimony, as to any matters of fact with which he was acquainted, or as to the common tradition of the churches. But in view of what Origen has said, how can we well suppose, that the opinion of Irenaeus, as recorded in Cont. Haeres, V. 30 was formed in any other way, than by his own interpretation of Revelation. 1:9". (1:281)

"Now it strikes me that Tertullian plainly means to class Peter, Paul, and John together, as having suffered at nearly the same time and under the same emperor. I concede that this is not a construction absolutely necessary; but I submit it to the candid, whether it is not the most probable." (1:284n.)

"It seems indisputably clear that the book of Revelation must be dated in the reign of Nero Caesar, and consequently before his death in June, AD68. He is the sixth king; the short-lived rule of the seventh king (Galba) has not yet come." (2:324)

"A majority of the older critics have been inclined to adopt the opinion of Irenaeus, viz., that it was written during the reign of Domitian, i.e., during the last part of the first century, or in AD95 or AD96. Most of the recent commentators and critics have called this opinion in question, and placed the composition of the book at an earlier period, viz., before the destruction of Jerusalem." (*A Commentary on the Apocalypse*, 2 vols; Andover, MD: Allen, Morrill, and Wardwell, 1845; p. 1:263)

"The manner of the declaration here seems to decide, beyond all reasonable appeal, against a later period than about AD67 or AD68, for the composition of the Apocalypse." (*A Commentary on the Apocalypse*, 2 vols; Andover, MD: Allen, Morrill, and Wardwell, 1845; p. 2:326)

Milton Terry (1898)

"...the trend of modem criticism is unmistakably toward the adoption of the early date of the Apocalypse." (***Biblical Apocalyptics*** p. 241n.)

"It is therefore not to be supposed that the language, or style of thought, or type of doctrine must needs resemble those of other production of the same author. .. The difference of language is further accounted for by the supposition that the apocalypse was written by the apostle at an early period of his ministry, and the gospel and epistles some thirty or forty years later." (ibid, p 255)

"A fair weighing of the arguments thus far adduced shows that they all excepting the statement of Irenaeus, favor the early rather than later date. The facts appealed to indicate the times before rather than after the destruction of Jerusalem." (*ibid, p* 258)

"Now, there is no contention that Galatians and Hebrews were written before the destruction of Jerusalem, and, to say the least, the most natural explanation of the allusions referred to is to suppose that the Apocalypse was already written, and that Paul and many others of his day were familiar with its contents. Writers who cite passages from the apostolic fathers to prove the priority of the Gospel of John are the last persons in the world who should presume to dispute the obvious priority of the Apocalypse of John to Galatians and Hebrews. For in no case are the alleged quotations of Gospel more notable or striking than these allusions to the Apocalypse in the New Testament epistles." (*ibid.,*260)

"The verb *was seen* is ambiguous and may be either it, referring to the Apocalypse, or *he*, referring to John himself." (*Biblical Hermeneutics*, p. 238)

C.Vanderwaal (1989)

"We cannot accept all the arguments of J.A.T. Robinson in his book *Redating the New Testament* (London, 1976), but we agree with his conclusion that all the books of the New Testament were written before the year AD70." (Cited in James E. Priest, "Contemporary Apocalyptic Scholarship and the Revelation," in *Johannie Studies: Essays in Honor of Frank Pack,* ed. James E. Priest; Malibu, CA: Pepperdine University Press; p. 199, n. 75)

"The book of Revelation presents a clear testimony to the churches in the first century. To be more specific, I am convinced that Revelation was written in the seventh decade of the first century – *before* the destruction of Jerusalem in the year 70, which Jesus talked about in Matthew 24." (*Hal Lindsey and Bible Prophecy*; St. Catharines, Ontario, Canada: Paideia Press, 1978; p. 12)

Appendix 4:

Commentaries on Matthew 24:14

The concept is that both Jews and Gentiles have the opportunity of receiving or rejecting Christ. The witness should be for or against them according to the use made of this opportunity. At least by implication here, the Gospel has been presented to the then known world which fulfils the prophecy by Jesus in Matthew 24:14. Jesus says "then the end shall come". Here is the question. What end is Jesus referring to? Let's look at several commentaries regarding Matthew 24:14. These are well respected writers and should help you to understand this passage regarding the Gospel being preached in the world. I will modify or shorten some of them for the sake of time. It will, in no way, change the meaning of the commentator.

Gill's Exposition of the Entire Bible

"And this Gospel of the kingdom, which Christ himself preached, and which He called and sent his apostles to preach, in all the cities of Judah; by which means men were brought into the kingdom of the Messiah. The Gospel shall be preached in all the world; not only in Judea, where it was now confined, and that by the express orders of Christ himself; but in all the nations of the world, for which the apostles had their commission enlarged, after our Lord's resurrection; when they were told to go into all the world, and preach the Gospel to every creature; and when the Jews put away the Gospel from them, they accordingly turned to the Gentiles; and before the destruction of Jerusalem, it was preached to all the nations under the heavens; and churches were planted in most places, through the ministry of it: and then shall the end come; not the end of the world, as the Ethiopic version reads it, and others understand it; but the end of the Jewish state, the end of the city and temple: so that the universal preaching of the Gospel all over the world, was the last criterion and sign, of the destruction of Jerusalem; and the account of that itself next follows, with the dismal circumstances which attended it."

Ellicott's Commentary for English Readers

"**Shall be preached in all the world.** The words must not be strained beyond the meaning which they would have for those who heard them, and they were certain to see in "all the world" (literally, *the inhabited earth,)* neither more nor less than the Roman empire; and it was true, as a matter of fact, that there was hardly a province of the empire in which the faith of Christ had not been preached before the destruction of Jerusalem. Special attention should be given to the words, "a witness unto all the *nations,"* *i.e.,* to all the Gentiles, as an implicit sanction of the work of which St. Paul was afterwards the great representative. So taken, the words prepare the way for the great mission. **Matthew 28:19.**

Let us give diligence to make our calling and election sure; then may we know that no enemy or deceiver shall ever prevail against us."

Barnes' Notes on the Bible

"And this Gospel of the kingdom shall be preached in all the world - The evidence that this was done is to be chiefly derived from the New Testament, and there it is clear. Thus Paul declares that it was preached to every creature under heaven **Colossians 1:6, Colossians 1:23**; that the faith of the Romans was spoken of throughout the whole world **Romans 1:8**; that he preached in Arabia Galatians 1:17, and at Jerusalem, and round about unto Illyricum **Romans 15:19**. We know also that He traveled through Asia Minor, Greece, and Crete; that he was in Italy, and probably in Spain and Gaul, **Romans 15:24-28.** At the same time, the other apostles were not idle; and there is full proof that within thirty years after this prophecy was spoken, churches were established in all these regions.

For a witness unto all nations - This preaching the Gospel indiscriminately to "all" the Gentiles shall be a proof to them, or a witness, that the division between the Jews and Gentiles was about to be broken down. Hitherto the blessings of revelation had been confined to the Jews. They were the special people of God. His messages had been sent to them only. When, therefore, God sent the Gospel to all other people, it was proof, or "a witness unto them," that the special Jewish economy was at an end.

Then shall the end come - The end of the Jewish economy; the destruction of the temple and city."

Matthew Poole's Commentary

"So said Mark, **Mark 13:10**. Some think that *the end* mentioned in the close of this verse refers to the destruction of Jerusalem; others, that it refers to the day of judgment. If we take *world* (as it is often taken) for the Gentiles in opposition to the Jews, the whole being put for a great part, it is most certain, that before Jerusalem was destroyed, the Gospel, which is here called the Gospel of the kingdom, either because it shows the way to the kingdom of God, or because it is that sacred instrument by which Christ draws men's hearts to himself, was preached to the world, that is, to the Gentiles, and that to a great part of them. Paul alone had carried it from Jerusalem to Illyricum. The Romans' faith was spoken of throughout the world, **Romans 1:8**. Paul said it was *preached to every creature,* Colossians 1:23 Romans 10:18 15:16 **Colossians 1:6 1 Timothy 3:16**. But others choose by *the end* here to understand the end of the world."

Matthew Henry's Concise Commentary and Jamieson-Fausset-Brown Bible Commentary as well as others indicate that this passage refers to a time prior to the destruction of Jerusalem in AD70.

Clarke's Commentary on Matthew 24:14

"And this Gospel of the kingdom shall be preached in all the world - But, notwithstanding these persecutions, there should be a universal publication of the glad tidings of the kingdom, for a testimony to all nations. God would have the iniquity of the Jews published everywhere, before the heavy stroke of his judgments should fall upon them; that all mankind, as it were, might be brought as witnesses against their cruelty and obstinacy in crucifying and rejecting the Lord Jesus. "In all the world", (Greek=oikoumene) Perhaps no more is meant here than the Roman empire; for it is beyond controversy that Luke 2:1, means no more than the whole Roman empire: as a decree for taxation or enrolment from Augustus Caesar could have no influence but in the Roman dominions; but see on Luke 2:1 (note). Tacitus informs us, Annal. I. xv., that, as early as the reign of Nero, the Christians were grown so numerous at Rome as to excite the jealousy of the government; and in other parts they were in proportion. However, we are under no necessity to restrain the phrase to the Roman empire, as, previously to the destruction of Jerusalem, the Gospel was not only preached in the lesser Asia, and Greece, and Italy, the greatest theatres of action then in the world; but was likewise propagated as far north as Scythia; as far south as Ethiopia; as far east as Parthia and India; and as far west as Spain and Britain. On this point, Bishop Newton goes on to say, That there is some probability that the Gospel was preached in the British nations by St. Simon the apostle; that there is much greater probability that it was preached here by St. Paul; and that there is an absolute certainty that it was planted here in the times of the apostles, before the destruction of Jerusalem. See his proofs. Dissert. vol. ii. p. 235, 236. edit. 1758. St. Paul himself speaks, **Colossians 1:6, Colossians 1:23**, of the Gospel's being come into "All The World", and preached "To Every Creature" under heaven. And in his Epistle to the Romans, **Romans 10:18**, he very elegantly applies to the lights of the church, what the psalmist said of the lights of heaven. Their sound went into all the earth, and their words unto the end of the world. What but the wisdom of God could foretell this, and what but the power of God could accomplish it?

Then shall the end come - When this general publication of the Gospel shall have taken place, then a period shall be put to the whole Jewish economy, by the utter destruction of their city and temple."

About the Contributor

Dan L. Young retired in 2014 after serving 43 years as an ordained pastor with the United Brethren in Christ church. He trusted Christ as his Savior at the age of sixteen and followed his calling to the ministry. He resides in Findlay, Ohio with his wife, Marilyn to whom he as been married 49 years. He is the father of two sons, five grandchildren, and one great granddaughter.

He graduated from Circleville Bible College in 1971 (now Ohio Christian University) with a Bachelor of Arts (B.A.). He received his Master of Theology (Th. M.) from International Theological Seminary (1983) and his Master of Divinity (M. Div) from Winebrenner Theological Seminary, Findlay, Ohio (2004).

He was awarded the Christian Service Award from Circleville Bible College in 1983. He has served his denomination in various capacities, including that as a Conference Superintendent. Dan spent his pastoral ministry in developing his three seminary specialties: Theology, Church History, and Church Growth.

He contributed most of the material in chapters 6, 7, 10 and 11 of this book and his input was invaluable in much of the rest.

About the Author

Doug Rolfe has had many experiences in his life which has helped shape his understanding of God's Word. Growing up on an 1800 acre farm in South Central Ohio, he learned about life, death, success, failure and how to apply the Bible to everyday living. From a very early age as he and his father milked cows together, his father would teach and mentor him in an effort to help him better understand Biblical truths. Doug always said he received his best education going to "cow college".

Doug attended Circleville Bible College to further his education and learn more about the Bible. It was there he saw different approaches to second coming prophecy and became very interested in pursuing eschatology. After reading many books and studying the Bible in depth, Doug realized that many of the doctrinal teachings regarding second prophecy he'd heard about were not Biblical and not what the Bible actually says about end-times prophecy. It has been his life-long dream to write this book to help you understand what he learned.

Doug is a retired enroute air traffic controller with his commercial pilot's license, instrument and multi-engine ratings, as well as a flight instructor license. He has taught large adult Sunday School classes for 30+ years and has written several Bible studies, has been a lead elder, board chairman, and treasurer of 3 churches across the years. After much study and attending a Creation College class, as well as other creation apologetic workshops, he is presently involved in teaching "creation apologetics" in a variety of settings. While he is a member of Mensa and continues to diligently study God's Word, none of his lifetime accomplishments compare to knowing his Lord intimately and looking steadily forward to His promise of eternal life with Him. Doug and his wife of nearly 48 years reside near Indianapolis, Indiana.

www.ingramcontent.com/pod-product-compliance
Lightning Source LLC
Chambersburg PA
CBHW022117080426

42734CB00006B/166